# Wine Room Construction

# Tips and Techniques

# Wine Room Construction Tips and Techniques

## By

## Taylor Michaels

Rev 2.0
Ch. 7 - Compressor Replacement Added

Construction activities can be hazardous. These hazards range from simply turning your body and something goes pop, putting you in great pain, to burning your house down in the middle of the night, while you are sleeping. In many places in the book, the author mentions specific safety concerns, but all construction activities should be conducted with safety in mind.

It has often been said in jest that 'real men don't read instructions,' but that is wrong. Real men want to be around and in good shape tomorrow and want their families, friends and neighbors to be around as well. Read and understand the instruction manual for each tool you buy. Then, put those manuals in a place where you can easily get them whenever you have a question about the operation of a particular tool.

Likewise, neither this book nor any other book will tell you everything you need to know about anything. A carved sign above my library bookcases says timeo homo unius libri, or 'Fear a man of one book.' A number of other excellent books are listed in the Appendix. These range from general house construction topics to details about each discipline. Each of these books is on my bookshelf and each has been valuable in educating me in building three additions to my house as well as the wine cellar. My bookshelf has many other books as well and those have all been useful. Further, I have consulted many sites on the web to obtain additional information. And last, of course, my Chemical Engineering education and decades of work have helped. But, I still don't know it all. You won't either, but you can learn enough to build a wine cellar you will be proud of -- safely.

Construction of a wine cellar can be a rewarding and instructive exercise and can lead to even bigger and more rewarding projects. Take your time and don't skip steps or take risks. If you don't understand something, get more information. If you can't do something, admit it and get help. Five years later, while you're sipping delicious wine with your dinner, you won't think any less of yourself. At night, when you wake up to that suspicious smell, you can confidently tell yourself it was that enchilada you had for dinner and not the money you should have spent on another book or on an electrician.

This is the second major version of this book. If you have any comments or corrections, please send them to the following:

tmichaelsbooks@yahoo.com.

Corrections will be incorporated (quickly). Also, check back from time to time. If you purchased the ebook and a new version of the ebook is published, send Amazon an email and they will allow you to download the new one for free. If you purchased the paperback, they will sell you the new ebook for ninety-nine cents.

# Table of Contents

**Chapter 1 - Introduction** — 1

**Chapter 2 - Why Build?** — 3
Why not build a wine room? — 7

**Chapter 3 - Major Design Considerations** — 11
Cost — 12
Who does what? — 15
Where? — 15
Wine Cellar Size — 20
Appearance — 24
Wine Racks — 33
Refrigeration — 45
Electrical — 63

**Chapter 4 - Design Details** — 67
Room Layouts — 68
Flooring — 71
Building the Room — 72
Refrigeration — 75

**Chapter 5 - Wine Cellar Construction** — 83
Building the Room — 83
Building Racks — 107
Refrigeration — 123
Electrical — 132
Flooring — 137
Tools — 150

**Chapter 6 - Operational Considerations** — 161
Temperature — 161
Refrigeration — 162
Numbering — 163
Loading — 164
Empty Spaces — 164

**Chapter 7 -Compressor Replacement** — 167
Preparation — 168
Disassembly — 169
Removing the compressor — 170
Reinstalling the New Compressor — 177
Startup — 178
Conclusion — 179

**Appendix** — 181
Wine Myths — 181

**Reference Books** — 185

# Chapter 1 - Introduction

The purpose of this book is to provide tips and techniques for planning and building your own wine room or wine cellar. Whether your wine room is small or large, the concepts are all the same. Also, believe it or not, much of the fun of building your own unique wine cellar is in the planning. A few layouts are included just to show some common possibilities, but even without a large amount of money, you can design and build a great cellar. A number of low cost options as well as some high-end options are discussed.

*Great Wine Cellar Potential*

This book is not a textbook on refrigeration or electrical work, but provides many useful insights. In addition, there may be local restrictions and codes on who can work on such items and, in some cases, building permits may be required. If you aren't sure, contact your local building inspectors to find out. If you hire out any part of your cellar construction, **make sure your contractor is licensed and bonded and any building permits required are actually obtained**.

The book is organized into three major sections: major design considerations, design details and wine cellar construction. The first two major sections are concerned with planning and the third with the actual construction of the room.

# Chapter 2 - Why Build?

Why should you build a wine room? If you are reading this book, you probably don't need a lecture on why you should proceed. You just need some encouragement and a few answers to questions you might be asking yourself or questions someone else might be asking you.

**1. Improves Dining.** Aged fine wine provides a far better dining experience and is more enjoyable than the raw young wine found in the stores. And we all know that wine aids digestion. The Bible says, "Drink no longer water, but use a little wine for thy stomach's sake." Recent studies show that wine, but not distilled spirits, helps counteract potentially harmful substances in meat.

**2. Convenience.** It is desirable to have close at hand an inventory of good wines to choose from because different foods require different wines to achieve their maximum enjoyment.

**3. Saves Money.** It is the least expensive way to be able to consume aged wine. In the long run, it is cheaper to build a wine cellar and fill it with young wine directly from the vintner than to buy old wines from a store. This cuts out the middleman and saves money. It also avoids wasting time on long internet searches trying to find them.

**4. Availability**. Sources of supply are not reliable. Just because a wine is in the store today does not mean it will be there in a few months and all your hard work and money spent in discovering a new wine will be wasted and lost because you can't find supplies or your new favorite. "It is necessary to kiss many frogs to find a prince." Good kisses should not be wasted.

**5. Saves More Money.** Wine is cheaper in quantity. Once you've saved that money, you don't want to lose it by carelessly storing it. You wouldn't keep lettuce in the oven, would you?

**6. Variety.** Variety is the spice of life. Having a large collection of wine insures a spicy life.

**7. Investment Value.** Fine wine not only improves with age, but becomes more valuable. Properly stored fine wine is a great investment.

*Vertical Row and X Box Racks*

4

**8. Teaches Valuable Skills.** Building your wine room teaches construction skills, which can later be used to build a house or fine furniture, especially when the racks are made from exotic wood like mahogany. Equipment purchased for wine cellar construction can later be used for house or furniture construction. (The cost of a table saw and other needed equipment would be much less than the cost of commercially made custom exotic wood racks.)

**9. Teaches Organization.** Using a wine cellar, as well as building a wine cellar, teaches and rewards organization and discourages disorder and sloppiness. Once you've purchased your prize wine, you want to easily find it.

**10. Great Souvenir.** Wine is an excellent souvenir to pick up on vacation. It does not fill up the clothes closet or require finding a place on the wall to hang it. Also, it doesn't look tacky once you've sobered up from that wonderful vacation.

**11. Collect Fine Art.** Wine labels are excellent examples of art. They can be removed and placed in books and used to impress all your friends as well as bringing back good memories, especially when you have traveled to wineries on vacation.

**12. Make Friends.** Wine is a great social facilitator. The bigger collection you have, the more friends you are likely to have and make. Also, wine tastings are an excellent way to meet new and interesting people.

**13. Make Many Friends.** Wine tastings are great fun. A vacation built around visiting different wineries can be educational and result in finding new and better wines to share with your friends back home. Once your collection of aged wine is built up, you can even host your own wine tastings for your friends. Throw in some cheese, nuts and chocolate and you could have some great parties.

# Why not build a wine room?

There are reasons why someone should not build a wine cellar, believe it or not.

**1. Health**. Sadly, as we age our tastes may change. It is possible that, if you are not in the best of health, something might happen which will prohibit you from consuming alcohol. Of course, the opposite is also true. Any number of things could happen which might cause you to want to increase your wine consumption -- greatly!

**2. Age.** At some age, the wisdom of inventorying ten years of wine which will not mature for ten years becomes questionable. At that time, you should begin to reduce your purchases, but only then.

*Wine Coolers for White Wine in Wine Room*

**3. Permanency.** In my life, I have lived in thirty-two houses. It would not have made any sense to spend time and money to build a room and fill it with expensive wine if I knew I would be moving in a few years. Although, I did move several cases of homemade wine several times. Maybe your company is likely to move you. It happened to me over and over. On the other hand, we all need to settle down at some time and make roots and a wine cellar.

**4. Home Sale.** A wine cellar may be a questionable financial addition to your house if you need to sell it quickly and soon. Most buyers, although saying how nice it looks and how beautiful it is, may think of the wasted space and possible maintenance costs. However, most buyers and all of their friends will secretly envy a person with a wine cellar, as it is such a great symbol of 'la dolce vita.' For some buyers, it will not add to the value of the house. But, for the right buyer, of course, it will add considerable value, especially if a small amount of aged wine is included in the sale.

*Vineyard in Bordeaux*

**5. Alternates.** In some cases, instead of a cellar, a large wine refrigerator may be better or maybe the use of rented storage is the right answer. However, a large wine refrigerator can be quite expensive and difficult to move around in your house and expensive to maintain. Also, one always takes a risk with rented storage. In addition, rented storage puts the wine an inconvenient distance away forcing you to plan your social activities well in advance, limiting your ability to change plans quickly.

The author hopes this section has helped clarify your thoughts on a wine room or cellar.

# Chapter 3 - Major Design Considerations

As you read this section, you will probably make decisions on the construction of your wine room. At some point, you may make a decision that violates previous decisions. Finish the chapter anyway, and then go back to the start and go through it again. Like most things in life and in construction, the final product will be the result of many compromises.

*Wine Press in Burgundy*

Major design considerations include, cost, aesthetics, shape and size, layout, location, style, ability, and the need to use what you have.

## Cost

As an engineer, I used to always begin each project with a blank sheet of paper and design the whole thing from scratch. At some point, however, I decided that some problems only had a few possible answers. It wasn't necessary to design and optimize every possibility, only the practical possibilities. Cost is a major factor in what is practical. By first asking yourself what is the maximum cost you would consider reasonable and then asking what you would really like to spend, you will narrow down the possibilities. Likewise, what is the maximum amount of time you would be willing to spend constructing your dream wine cellar? And, of course, you have to decide what you are capable of doing, what you are capable of learning and what are you neither able to do nor want to do. Those answers will bracket the range of possible actions and designs.

The simplest and least expensive space for a wine cellar is in an existing room, whether upstairs or in the basement. If you have a bird leaving your nest (or being pushed out), converting that room to a wine cellar is not only the least expensive way to have a wine cellar, but it makes a return to the nest either less practical or more difficult. By converting an existing room into a wine cellar, no walls have to be built, no floor has to be covered and no ceiling has to be constructed. All you need to add is air conditioning, insulation of inside walls, wine racks and wine. The whole thing could easily be done in a week with purchased racks.

In the case of a large upstairs room, adding thousands of pounds of wine may cause structural problems. Unless you are confident of the structural integrity of the floor support system, it may be wise to maximize wine racks along the walls of the room and put no large quantities in the center. If you later move from the house, you can take your racks and your

AC. The only thing left behind and wasted is insulation in a few walls.

The main costs for this option would be for insulation, AC and racks. At the low end of less than 1000 bottles, insulation would be around $50, with a through-the-window AC for $80. Racks would vary from nothing for boxes on the floor to $400 for low-end commercial wire racks, $600 for DIY racks of maple to $1600 for DIY racks of mahogany or walnut. Commercial rack kits could cost from $2.50 per square foot to over $10 per square foot. For a 1000 bottle cellar with eight bottles per square foot, the wine cellar would have 125 square feet of wine. That would be $300 to over $1000 for a low-end kit. A prebuilt custom system of more expensive wood could cost over $10,000. A number of companies sell kits and provide design services. Check these out on the internet for the latest prices and material availability. The choices today are far greater than they were a year ago.

*Architectural Elements*

For a room constructed in the basement, the materials for the room itself would cost around $500 for a 1000 bottle cellar. Also, a through-the-wall or window-type AC could be used, exhausting heat into the basement. If a basement window were available and the AC could be placed there, the wine cellar would not heat up the basement in the summer. On the other hand, it wouldn't heat the basement in the winter, either. This may be a case where the pros and the cons are about equal and a through-the-wall AC in the basement exhausting heat to the basement is the best answer. Such a unit could cost less than $100. A through-the-wall, self-contained unit designed for wine cellars could cost $500 to $1000 and presumably would last longer and be able to reach lower temperatures, although the data on reliability is not conclusive.

A split unit may also be used with the compressor located in the basement or outside the house. Split units can be surprisingly expensive with costs starting at over $1000 for a smaller unit. If one were somewhat enterprising and more than average handy with a soldering torch, one could take apart two small window units, add a hundred dollars worth of copper tubing (which would be required with the commercial split unit, anyway) and make one DIY split unit for a couple hundred dollars. As long as the units used 134a refrigerant, the job would not be impossible for an amateur.

As a final point, if you have a larger cellar, then your wine investment could be considerable. With two thousand bottles at even twenty dollars per bottle, that's a forty thousand dollar investment in wine. At fifty dollars per bottle, one hundred thousand dollars. Although the cooling units are expensive, they are cheap compared to your investment in wine. The conclusion is that anyone with a larger cellar or more expensive wine should consider having two installed coolers, especially with split units, which are difficult to service. If you use a through-the-wall unit, then having a spare unit sitting around may not be a bad alternate, but having a second installed unit set one degree higher than the first, and with the fan set to only come on with the compressor was on, would be better insurance, especially with a split unit.

## Who does what?

In deciding who will do the work, you should realistically assess your own abilities, tools, available time and previous experience in learning new skills from books and the internet. Some people cannot learn manual skills from a book. They have to practice on some learning exercise first. On the other hand, a wine cellar is a good small construction project that can teach the variety of skills needed to build your own furniture or even build a new house or a major addition to your existing house.

Construction may involve building insulated walls, installing wiring and lighting and installing some type of cooling system. Which of these you should do yourself depends on your skills and your ability to learn. This book will not give anyone all the knowledge necessary to do any of these, but will point out the major items of importance. It would be wise to obtain separate books on each skillset that the builder needs to develop. A number of books I have used are listed in the Appendix. In some cases, even if you do not feel comfortable doing all of one type of work, it may be possible for the amateur to do some of the work, like running refrigeration lines and setting the AC units in place while hiring a professional to do the final tie-ins and pressurize the system. Similarly, you could run electrical cable runs and leave the tie-ins to an electrician.


## Where?

Where you locate your wine cellar has a great bearing on the cost as well as the convenience of using the cellar. The best location is a combination of cost, convenience, quality, size, availability of space and others. A true wine cellar many feet below the ground is not practical for most people and would require extensive excavation and serious attention to drainage. (Don't ever forget drainage when building something

15

below grade level.) Such a cellar may not even be possible in many locations. My property has so many rocks that every time I dig a hole, I worry I've hit bedrock after a foot of digging.

*A Diagonal Corner*

**Existing Room**

As stated previously, use of an existing room is the easiest and cheapest option. The only thorny issue has to do with insulation. It is not difficult to remove the drywall on one side of a wall and add insulation with a vapor barrier and then put new drywall back on. That would be the recommended procedure.

It is even possible to add insulation to an existing wall by cutting a six-inch high horizontal slot in the drywall across the width of a wall about four feet above the floor. Then faced insulation could be shoved up through the stud cavity above the slot and down into the stud cavity below. The drywall removed could then be replaced, taped, mudded, primed and painted. For a single wall, this should only take a few hours. Some might say that this system would not be ideal, but others might say it would be adequate.

## Under the Stairs

Putting a wine cellar under the stairs seems a difficult task because space is severely limited and access to cooling is difficult. I once opened up the area under a set of stairs for storage and that was not difficult, but the amount of space available was small. Obviously, insulation would have to be added and some way of keeping the insulation in place would be needed. Existing stud bays could be used for insulation bats and a layer of drywall added over that would protect the insulation from being damaged by wine boxes or bottles. Insulation would also be required under the stairs. Two-inch Styrofoam sheets would provide an R value of 10, which might be adequate, but three inches of foam would be better. The Styrofoam could be screwed to the bottom of the steps and the joints taped.

The hard part of an under-stairs wine room would be providing cooling. If the house had a basement, then the cooling system could be installed in the basement and ducts run to and from the cellar to provide cooling. I once installed an air conditioner in the ceiling of a garage and ran ducts to the backside of the AC unit to provide outside air to the condenser. That worked, but a supplementary duct fan or blower would be a desirable addition.

Also, if a crawl space were available, then an AC could be situated there and ducts run to the wine cellar. The outside side of an AC in a crawlspace would probably become filled with dust and would have to be hosed out from time to time. I've done that, too. (What can I say, I'm addicted to AC.) Ducting the outside of the AC to outside air through a foundation wall would solve the dust problem, but the air inlets would have to be protected from bees and a duct fan or two would be needed.

Commercial ducted coolers are available, but are not cheap. Adding ducts to a window AC would be much less expensive. Obviously, the warranty would be void, but it would not cost much to get a new one. Keeping the wine at fifty-five degrees with a window AC would probably not be possible without a tremendous amount of insulation. However, sixty degrees is feasible and would probably be satisfactory, especially for red wines.

## Attic

People on TV shows have put a wine cellar in the attic. It sounds odd, but it's theoretically possible. If, in this arrangement, the walls should then be subject to attic temperatures on the outside, it would be wise to use much more insulation. You might get away with R19 (6 inches of fiberglass) in the walls if you have a larger cooler. Moving to R30 (10 inches) would be necessary if you live in a warmer climate. If one of the walls of the attic wine cellar would be a gable wall and a through-the-wall AC could be installed, then a much higher capacity AC could be used to fight the heat. Its cost would then not be great. Again, using a window AC might limit the wine cellar to sixty degrees.

## Basement

Other than digging a hole under the house or in the front yard, the next best location might be a basement in the deepest most northeast end. A basement, finished or not, provides several benefits including lots of space and lower temperatures. The downside is the possibility of an irregular ceiling full of pipes, ducts and wires. There are many benefits to having a totally enclosed and insulated room, including improved security, reduced cooling investment and operating cost and reduced temperature variation. To get these benefits, it would be necessary to install a ceiling or use the existing floor joists as ceiling joists. The best location in the basement may be the northeast corner or maybe the deepest corner to get the lowest temperature and the most consistent temperature. However, an unobstructed ceiling is desirable and existing occupants of the basement, clothes washer and dryer or others, may already have staked out the best locations. Construction is always a matter of compromise and the best location in the basement will be a compromise of all these and other factors.

**Outbuilding**

Some people have installed their wine cellar in a shed detached from their house, frequently partially below the ground. The requirements are similar to building a room in the house, but the cooling requirements could be greater, prompting the need for greater insulation and a bigger cooling unit. Building the shed partially underground, like a root cellar, would help reduce cooling requirements. In the winter, the space may require heating. This is also the case in winter for some people building their wine cellar in the basement. Instead of a standard window AC unit, in this case, a window or through-the-wall heat pump unit would be needed. The heat pump design would decrease heating cost in the winter, over the use of a strip heater, and would take only a little more space than a normal AC. I use such a unit in my workshop and it has worked well. It is somewhat similar to units in some hotel rooms. By getting a unit of the type and form factor used by hotels, the unit would be cheaper and obtaining replacement units would be easier because of the standardization of sizes and mass production of this type of unit. Cost of a window heat pump would be around $500.


**Control**

As will be mentioned elsewhere, wine cellars are largely about control. Control involves security, temperature, humidity, darkness and vibration. Although little data is available, it is widely believed that consistency of all of these is important. Many of these will be dealt with later, but control of vibration should not be overlooked. The wine cellar location should not be an area where excessive vibration occurs. Placing a wine collection below a stairway where people are constantly stomping up and down seems questionable. Likewise, locating it where a motor or fan will cause vibration should be avoided. Some say the reason to worry about vibration is that solids settle out of the wine and that is made difficult by vibration. Possibly more important, agitation accelerates most chemical reactions, in this case leading to 'premature aging,' although again, little data is available.

## Wine Cellar Size

Developing a layout, like many things, is a compromise between cost and benefit. And somewhere in the equation comes need and availability of space. The bigger the wine cellar, the greater the cost in money for construction materials, money for cooling equipment and, of course, money for wine to fill it (unless you make your own and have a big cask, like a guy I ran across in Stuttgart.)

*Party Time in Stuttgart.*

If availability of space is not a problem, then the first step is to figure out how much space you need. One consideration is short-term storage versus long-term storage. In my case, I don't keep any significant inventory of port, although I do drink it often. The port we drink is aged ten or twenty years in the cask and further aging in the bottle is not believed to be important. So, for port, we trek to the Total Wines store nearby once every month and pick up a supply. Likewise, many white wines do not age well beyond four years. The following chart docs the simple math of bottles per week times weeks per year times number of years of storage. If for example, you drink one bottle of white per week, stored four years, and one bottle of red, stored ten years, then the total is 208 plus 624 or 832 bottles. Add in a dozen bottles of port, or other short-term storage, and you have a need for 844 bottles.

| | | Years | | | | |
|---|---|---|---|---|---|---|
| | | 4 | 6 | 8 | 10 | 12 |
| | 1 | 208 | 312 | 416 | 520 | 624 |
| | 2 | 416 | 624 | 832 | 1040 | 1248 |
| B | 3 | 624 | 936 | 1248 | 1560 | 1872 |
| p | 4 | 832 | 1248 | 1664 | 2080 | 2496 |
| W | 5 | 1040 | 1560 | 2080 | 2600 | 3120 |
| | 6 | 1248 | 1872 | 2496 | 3120 | 3744 |
| | 7 | 1456 | 2184 | 2912 | 3640 | 4368 |
| | 8 | 1664 | 2496 | 3328 | 4160 | 4992 |

*Bottles Required*

The chart also serves to help provide an estimate of the capital requirement for the wine. If wine is twenty dollars per bottle and you drink one per week and age it for ten years, you need five hundred twenty bottles or over ten thousand dollars of wine.

Once the storage need is established, the size of the room can be calculated. If the entire room is done with vertical racks at 8.8 bottles per square foot, then we need 844 bottles divided by 8.8 bottles per square foot or 96 square feet of rack. With a room height of 8 feet, and with six inch moldings at the top and four inch at the bottom, we have a usable height of 7 feet

2 inches or 7.17 ft. That means a racking length about 13 feet of rack. The room would be 6'6" long by 5 feet wide inside allowing for bottles one foot wide and three feet of walking space. Or 4 feet wide if you are willing to be a little cramped. The following chart provides an estimate of the wine cellar size for the parameters above, for estimating purposes.

## Wine Cellar Size for Estimating Purposes
### Sizes in Feet for One Layout

|   |   | Years | | | | |
|---|---|---|---|---|---|---|
|   |   | **4** | **6** | **8** | **10** | **12** |
|   | **1** | 4 x 4 | 4 x 5 | 4 x 6 | 4 x 7 | 4 x 8 |
|   | **2** | 5 x6 | 5 x 8 | 5 x 9 | 5 x 11 | 5 x 13 |
|   | **3** | 5 x 8 | 5 x 11 | 5 x 14 | 9 x 8 | 9 x 10 |
| **B** | **4** | 5 x 9 | 4 x 13 | 9 x 9 | 9 x 11 | 9 x 13 |
| **p** | **5** | 5 x 11 | 9 x 9 | 9 x 10 | 9 x 13 | 11 x 13 |
| **W** | **6** | 5 x 13 | 8 x 10 | 9 x 13 | 11 x 13 | 11 x 15 |
|   | **7** | 9 x 8 | 9 x 11 | 11 x 13 | 11 x 14 | 11 x 17 |
|   | **8** | 9 x 9 | 9 x 12 | 11 x 13 | 11 x 16 | 11 x 18 |

Following is a simple layout for a small wine cellar to show some of the complexities in developing and optimizing the design.

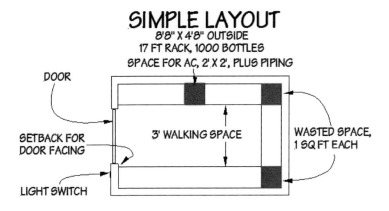

# SIMPLE LAYOUT
## 8'8" X 4'8" OUTSIDE
## 17 FT RACK, 1000 BOTTLES
## SPACE FOR AC, 2' X 2', PLUS PIPING

DOOR

SETBACK FOR
DOOR FACING

3' WALKING SPACE

WASTED SPACE,
1 SQ FT EACH

LIGHT SWITCH

For those not flush with money, efficiency is important. For the simple rectangular layout above, you can see that a certain amount of wasted space exists in the corners. Intuitively, one might think that angling the corners would use some of that space, but as the layout below shows, intuition is not correct. Although a small amount of previously unused space is now used (in green) a much larger unused space results. Thus, the efficiency of the alternate layout is not as good and fewer bottles can be stored.

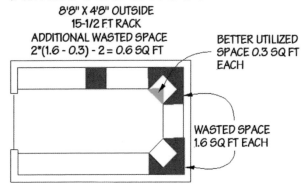

# ALTERNATE LAYOUT
## 8'8" X 4'8" OUTSIDE
## 15-1/2 FT RACK
## ADDITIONAL WASTED SPACE
## 2*(1.6 - 0.3) - 2 = 0.6 SQ FT

BETTER UTILIZED
SPACE 0.3 SQ FT
EACH

WASTED SPACE
1.6 SQ FT EACH

The alternate layout, however, is esthetically more pleasing and looks more upscale than the simple one above.

23

Additional wasted space results from having to have a cooling system. As the cooling system requires a drain, power lines, and, possibly, refrigeration lines, then provision must be made for these. If they are provided for before the walls are built, they can be enclosed in the walls. (For a through-the-wall unit, that works, but for a split unit, maintenance could require removing the unit and building the refrigerant lines into the wall could be a mistake.) A small amount of space is also required for door facings unless a modern style of architecture is used. Putting the light switch outside avoids the need to use wall space inside for that as well. In these layouts, no space is provided for an electrical outlet.

In the alternate layout, some of the wasted space could be utilized if the owner had need for storing larger bottles, such as magnums. The racks could be made deeper and wider. That appearance would be even better.

**Location of cooler**
The drawing shows the cooler on the long sidewall instead of the end wall. For coolers where the outlet air vent points the air in two directions, this is preferred. If the outlet air flows straight out of the cooler to the front, a location on the end wall might be preferred. Also, many manufacturers recommend the cooler be placed high in the room as cold air naturally sinks. It would be best in any case to make sure that the exit air does not directly impinge on any bottles, as this would cause undesirable temperature fluctuations. If some impingement cannot be avoided, some kind of baffle should be fabricated to divert the cold air into empty space. It may be possible to bend the louvers on the exit grill to help divert the air away from bottles.

# Appearance
The appearance of the cellar says something about the owner as much as the wine. If you are a logical and no-frills sort of person, then boxes on the floor or simple wire racks may convey an appearance you are happy with.

*Simple Wire Racks*

On the other hand, if you want an appearance of opulence and luxury, it would be good to include a number of architectural elements and interesting lighting fixtures in your cellar.

## DINING ROOM

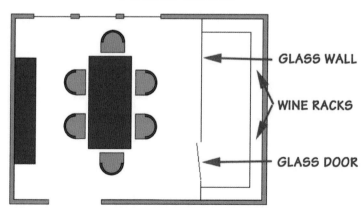

In searching the internet while researching for this book, I ran across companies specializing in wine rooms with one side made of glass. In some cases, the wine cellar was an extension of a living room or a dining room with a glass wall separating the two. This certainly provides an upscale look, although only with upscale racks.

This design also brings into question the idea that wine cellars should not have glass in the doors. The pictures shown did not have any condensation on the glass and the glass in my door does not either. That is probably because the wine cellar is not cold enough.

### Architecture

Even a relatively small wine room can have interesting architectural elements

*Arched End of Cellar*

Adding this arch to the end of the room required only a small loss of space. Refrigerators were installed below the granite countertop to handle some better white wines.

The bluish light comes from an LED strip behind the front of the arch. Note that the inside of the arch is made of strips of wood somewhat reminiscent of barrel staves.

*Barrel Stave Arch with LED Strip*

The white strip is the actual LED strip which runs on 12 volts DC provided by a wall transformer which sits on top of the refrigerators below the granite slab.

Along the right side of this wine cellar is a bump-out which serves as another architectural element and costs no bottles and very little wood.

*Bump Out on One Side of Wine Cellar*

27

Note the black molding at the pictures above and below, below the crown molding. It is painted poplar and adds another element to the architecture.

*Angled Vertical Racks*

Entering the wine cellar and turning around we can see another architectural element. This is an angled set of vertical racks in the corner of the room. In addition to architectural interest, this provides a considerable amount of stiffness to the entire rack system in this area. Even if the racks had not been attached to the wall with screws, it is unlikely this portion would ever tip over. To the right side can be seen a two-inch bulkhead with a flat panel on the side. The black poplar crown molding detail can also be seen. (Before building crown moldings at odd angles, do some research and have a good supply of aspirin and test boards. Another book could be written about that subject.)

*Architectural Features*

In the above picture can be seen more of the bulkhead and end panel. To the right is a forty-five degree angle in the wall where the door is located. This is another architectural element and cost only a few bottles in capacity. The door facings and jambs are of solid mahogany. The bamboo pattern in the door can be seen also.

### Style

With regard to style, many types of wine racks are available commercially and many more can be custom built.

Racks and walls made of concrete, by themselves, would not be considered stylish, but the vision of thousands and thousands of bottles is certainly impressive and for that reason they have a style. If the purpose of style is to impress, then the racks above are stylish. They would be more stylish, I think, in mahogany or other nice wood, but they are impressive, none-the-less.

We have all seen pictures of racks made of sewer pipe or flue pipe and, by themselves, they look cheap and unattractive.

29

But in a setting of exotic wood and good lighting, they can add an element of variety to a wine cellar.

*Concrete Racks in Burgundy*

When I first moved into my current house, I installed wire racks in the utility room with a window AC to keep it cool until the wine cellar could be completed. Those were not attractive, but were necessary. Using one of those racks in a wine cellar might, however, be interesting if surrounded by nice wood or stone.

Style in some cases relates to variety and the best arrangement of a variety of things. Spending a vast amount of money on items with no additional function is not always required. Imagination is important and a long look through Google Images will provide many unusual ways to improve the style of your cellar.

Other pictures of wine cellars show different ceiling treatments. Crown molding is one easy element to add, but some cellars had ceilings of wood or stone. Wood would not be that hard to install. A layer of plywood could be screwed to the ceiling joists and wood strip flooring attached to that with finishing nails and construction adhesive. Engineered wood strip flooring of a half-inch or three-eighths-inch thickness might be a good choice as it looks good and is light. If I were doing that, I would use a lot of screws, nails and adhesive.

## Space

Space itself is not stylish, but it is an enabler of style. However, space does affect appearance. The more space you have, the more types of interesting architecture you can add. It has often been observed that one of the most obvious signs of opulence is wasted space. The previous design would look more opulent had the center section been larger. Obviously, an eight by ten wine cellar would look more opulent and a bigger cellar would be even richer looking, all else being the same. The wine room mentioned previously with a glass wall wastes the wall space, but it is unquestionably opulent.

For some unusual designs, check out the following web site:

http://www.winecellarinnovations.com/ideas/popularideas/Glass-Enclosed-Wine-Cellars/

## Light

A tremendous variety of light fixtures is available to light the wine cellar. A trip through the local building supply store would be a good place to start looking. Beyond that, are many lighting supply businesses on the internet. Literally thousands of different fixtures are available. It might be a good idea to plan on several fixtures, large and small. The bulb size of each can be adjusted to get the lighting desired in the place desired. Although wine cellar lights would be turned on only a short amount of time each day, I still advocate using LED or florescent bulbs to minimize excess heat and to protect against the occasional mistake of leaving the lights on. Both are available in a range of light colors and sizes.

Should an existing room with an existing window be used as a wine cellar, it is desirable to minimize the light entering through the window, as sunlight is generally believed to contribute to the deterioration of wine. If a window air conditioner is used, then part of the window is blocked by the AC unit. Covering the remainder with a few sheets of

31

insulation would reduce both the light and the heat coming through the window. Insulation sheets are available with reflective aluminum foil on one side, which would help reduce solar heating. This would be a good choice for one of the layers of insulation covering the window.

For the wine cellar designs where one wall is glass, the question of unwanted light is open. If the wine room is part of a dining room and the room is only used for an hour or so per day, then excess light may not be a problem. It is also possible to get various types of coating on glass to reduce ultraviolet light, which is probably the worst offender.

## Wood

Wooden wine racks are common in wine cellars that are more stylish and can be made from a variety of wood species. Although pine, redwood and mahogany have often been used, virtually anything else which can be milled, including PVC and metals, can be made into wine racks. Many of the racks are made of large flat sections and for these, plywood faced with a thin veneer of an exotic wood is usually less expensive than using solid exotic wood. For example, mahogany boards from my local lumberyard cost around $5.50 per square foot whereas mahogany veneered half-inch plywood costs around $3.00 per square foot. If the edges of the plywood are to be visible, they should be covered with something, either a face frame or homemade or commercially produced veneer strips of the same wood. The veneer can be made from scrap pieces of solid wood and hence would have no out-of-pocket cost. It is recommended that the wood be finished with varnish or a similar water and alcohol resistant finish to resist bottle leakage or, sadly, a broken bottle.

If you are friendly with the folks at your local lumberyard, it might be possible to get scraps from them free. Some lumberyards have branched out from just selling rough lumber to making and selling moldings. Many of the leftover pieces are bigger than one by one and could be used for the horizontal pieces (rails) of a vertical wine rack.

When I first started thinking about a wine cellar, the choices of commercial wooden wine racks were minimal and expensive. Recently, however, a great variety of racks have become available, some light-colored wood racks are as cheap as $2.50 per square foot or around twenty-five cents per bottle. Before purchasing any commercial racks, make sure you understand all the assembly requirements. Some may involve getting a heavy box full of 'Lincoln logs' and having to nail and glue them together yourself from a detailed set of plans. This would require purchase of a small nail gun and a compressor with days of construction time necessary. Others may come completely built and finished. Know before you buy.

## Wine Racks

A great variety of styles of wine rack styles have been developed including, vertical and horizontal racks and rectangular, X and diamond boxes.

*Functional, But Not Pretty*

Racks are also made from heavy steel wire and even sewer pipe, PVC pipe and flue tiles are used. Ordinary shelf units are essentially larger rectangular boxes. In all cases, racks should be attached to the wall. Wood should not placed in direct contact with a concrete floor, but should be separated by an impervious moisture barrier (a piece of plastic).

**Vertical Rows**

Vertical rows are some of the most common racks and a cellar without these looks like it's missing something.

*A Combination of Styles*

Having said that, vertical rows are not as efficient as boxes for mass storage and are much more tedious and time consuming to build. Vertical rows are excellent for storing varieties that are only available as a few bottles. Rather than wasting a whole box section, the last few of a box of wine can be transferred to vertical rows, making room for another box. Also, sorting through a box of different bottles to find one bottle is not fun and could result in breakage as well as agitating the bottles. Storing bottles of different shape is dangerous and can be hazardous to the wine. Rows are generally made from solid wood and are expensive in terms of material and, especially, labor.

If all of your bottles appear to be the same size, it would still be wise to build three different sizes of racks that vary by around a quarter of an inch with only a few of the larger and smaller sizes. Then, if in the future, you get some odd sized bottles, you will have a good place to put them. If you don't, then only normal size bottles (whatever that is) will fit.

## VERTICAL ROW

22-1/4" x 40-1/4"

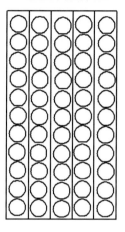

55 BOTTLES
8.8 B/SQ FT

Before building vertical rows, measure the size of the wine bottles in your collection. Although they all look about the same, they vary by over a quarter of an inch for full-sized bottles. I measured four bottles and they were all the same size. I made the rows with only one eighth of an inch of clearance and some of my larger bottles will not fit. Some of these ended up going into an X Box and others into a row that, by chance, ended up a little wide. Another two of my rows ended up a quarter of an inch smaller than the design and these are now used to house 500 ml bottles and port bottles. Thankfully, there were only two rows.

Construction of the racks is tedious and time consuming, and several jigs were made to simplify the construction process. These are shown in a later section.

*Vertical Rows & X Boxes*

With all the open area, vertical racks have better air circulation than the box racks and should have more even temperatures.

**Horizontal Row**

Racks patterned in a horizontal row are the least space efficient and are mainly used for display. Many variations are possible, some with the bottles all facing the same direction and some with the bottles alternating.

## HORIZONTAL ROW

## 8 BOTTLES
## 4.4 B/SQ FT

Horizontal rows are good for showing wine labels and could be a good choice for those expensive and rare bottles in your collection. But these racks are of low efficiency and mainly good for individual bottles of each wine. Another choice would be to line up what was to be consumed for the next week to make it simple for your significant other to easily pick one.

*Horizontal Row Variation*

These racks are easy to build, but require a band saw or jig saw with subsequent significant sanding. A drum sander would be helpful, but one rack would not justify buying a drum sander. (It is possible to get a cheap sanding drum kit for an electric drill.) The racks are made from solid wood, but it might be possible to use plywood with a thin commercial veneer to cover the edges. Horizontal row racks should provide for good air circulation.

**Boxes**

Boxes are made generally from plywood, which can be veneered plywood in many different exotic wood species. Boxes could be made from solid wood, glued into panels, if you have lots of money. They are easier to build than vertical rows, but use of a box for different size bottles is not a good idea as you may have to sort through many to get what you want. Also, stacking different size bottles in one box section may result in instability with bottles falling out. Trust me on that. Likewise, use of boxes without a front, is probably not a good idea in earthquake-prone areas. Air circulation in boxes is not as good as in vertical rows, but if the room is well insulated and a fan runs continuously, that should not be a problem.

### Rectangular Box Design

The rectangular box design is the most efficient layout and the easiest to build. In most of the wineries I have visited this arrangement was used, sometimes made from concrete as indicated before.

As the diagram below shows, the rectangular box holds over eleven bottles per square foot and as the photos below show they do not have to look as bad as the concrete bins above. For the maximum stability, it is necessary to build the boxes with only a small amount of excess space. The layout shown below is not as efficient as the one in the picture because rows are staggered, but it is more stable.

## RECTANGULAR BOX
## 21-3/4" x 13-1/16"

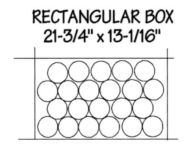

## 22 BOTTLES
## 11.1 B/SQ FT

Note in the picture below, a face frame covers the plywood between the upper X Boxes and the lower Rectangular Boxes. The two sets were built as a unit.

*Rectangular and X Boxes*

The plywood edges were hidden by using the face frame for top bottom and sides and by handmade mahogany veneer on the vertical and X section pieces. That veneer was cut to the width of the plywood and one-eighth of an inch in thickness using a table saw.

## X Box Design
The X Box has decent space efficiency and has a look that most people like. The boxes can be built in a horizontal as well as vertical layout.

# SQUARE BOX
## 25" SQUARE

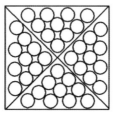

# 40 BOTTLES
# 9.2 B/SQ FT

In the photo following, the box has a face frame covering the horizontal and vertical edges with shop made eighth-inch thick veneer covering the X sections. The boxes stop at a height that allows a single vertical piece of mahogany to cover the gap between the box and the crown molding set.

*Vertical X Boxes*

The horizontal X boxes below were built together with the rectangular boxes below them as a single unit, saving one piece of plywood.

*X and Rectangular Boxes Built as One Unit*

To the left of the picture one can see the granite counter top and one of the refrigerators used for white wines.

## Diamond Box Design

The diamond-shaped box design is visually appealing, but appears to have several drawbacks. In the first design, below, the corner sections hold only four bottles, which could be useful, but the center section, to be fully functional, contains twenty-five bottles, or over two cases, and would probably be unstable with so many bottles. In addition, it appears to be less sturdy as the inside box relies on nails and glue to stay in place and does not reinforce the outer square box.

41

# DIAMOND BOX

## 25" SQUARE

# 41 BOTTLES
# 9.8 B/SQ FT

The second design hold the same number of bottles, but has less bottles per section, with nine in one section, seven in four sections and one bottle in four other sections. This would be more practical and more stable as well. Construction would still be more difficult than an X box as the internal sections would have to be notched twice whereas the X box design is only notched once. The diagonal pieces would be held in place with only nails and glue unless dadoes are used, which adds more complication. Obviously, more dividers could be added and more sections created. In that case, it may be wise to make the box an inch or so wider to take care of the extra wood. Any design should be laid out on paper or on the computer to make sure space is not being wasted.

# DIAMOND BOX 2
## 25" SQUARE

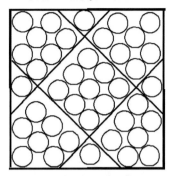

# 41 BOTTLES
# 9.8 B/SQ FT

**How to Decide**

So, given all the choices, how does one decide what style of rack to use? Part of the answer is simple and part is not. First, if your collection is made of a small number of bottles of a large variety of wines, say three or four bottles each, then vertical racks are ideal. You can go directly to the bottle you want without disturbing any other bottles. Construction takes more time and is more tedious, but air circulation is excellent and ease of selection is the best.

If your collection is all of full or nearly full boxes, then the box racks are a good bet. On the other hand, after a few years, your full boxes will not be full anymore. My solution was to have about half my storage in vertical racks and the other half in boxes. For the sake of style, a variety of boxes can be used, but the X boxes and square boxes favor larger numbers of bottles per section while the diamond boxes favor smaller numbers. So again, a split between the three might be reasonable. Also, as square boxes can be made almost any size, they can be used to 'make up' the remaining dimensions after 'optimum-sized' X boxes and diamond boxes are laid out.

43

Looking back at my wine cellar, I wish I had made some diamond boxes. At the time of construction, I thought they would take too much time to build and might not be as stable. But they seem to have more style and they favor half-boxes of wine.

Following is a typical rack layout for a ten-foot-long wall. This provides a variety of 'batch sizes' for your different wines. The three diamond boxes on the left along with the rectangular box below could be built as one unit. Likewise the X boxes and rectangular boxes below them can be built as one unit. The vertical racks could also be built as a single unit. For my cellar, I screwed two by fours to the floor first and then set the boxes on them. Later, the base moldings were attached. Note that the appearance is enhanced by keeping some lines consistent across the width of the room.

TYPICAL RACK LAYOUT
8' X 10'
550 BOTTLES

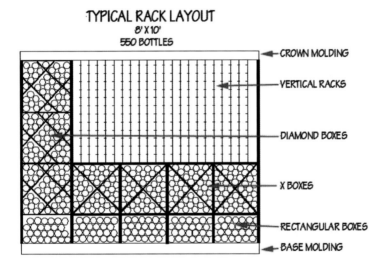

CROWN MOLDING

VERTICAL RACKS

DIAMOND BOXES

X BOXES

RECTANGULAR BOXES

BASE MOLDING

In any such layout, it is wise to draw the layout in detail on the wall before starting construction of the racks. That way, any small layout errors can be found before any expensive mistakes are made.

## Refrigeration

To refrigerate or not to refrigerate, that is the question. Most of the answer lies in two facts. First, some people live where it is rarely over eighty degrees and second, refrigeration equipment is expensive. When I moved to Missouri, many people said the house they were trying to sell me didn't have air conditioning because "we don't need it here." I heard the same thing when I moved to Virginia. They were both wrong.

If you really don't want refrigeration, then commit yourself to using a lot of insulation. Loads of it. Twelve inches of fiberglass or six inches of spray foam as a minimum. Then your cellar will tend to operate somewhere between the annual average temperature and the daily average temperature of the spot where you build it. The more insulation you use, the closer it will get to the annual average temperature at that point. My personal opinion is that your wine will benefit from some kind of temperature control. If the place you put it gets colder than desired, then that temperature control may include heating. As I previously asked, you wouldn't store lettuce in the oven, would you? And of course, you wouldn't store lettuce in the freezer either.

In my first wine cellar, three walls were exposed to the outside temperatures and I put a window AC in one window to control the temperature. Fortunately, the room had an AC vent. In spring and fall, I taped it over. In winter, I removed half the tape and let in just enough hot air from the furnace to keep the cooler working. In summer, I took the tape off. The thermometer never showed a temperature variation of more than one degree from the sixty-degree control point.

Refrigeration can be one of the major costs of a wine cellar, especially with a split unit. Also, installing your own split unit requires either outside help or purchase of equipment unlikely to ever be used for anything else. These are a vacuum pump, a set of refrigeration gauges and a propane torch. The total cost of this equipment is less than $200 and although that is cheaper than hiring the job out, the tools may never be used again. For this reason, use of single (self-contained) units is cheaper and easier. The single unit installation only requires

45

setting the unit into a window or into a custom opening in the wall of the wine cellar and possibly locating an outlet nearby.

Some makers of wine coolers say that their units don't last long because they are operating seventy percent of the time. I don't know if that is true, but insulation is the key to keeping refrigeration needs low. Instead of four-inch-thick walls, you could have six inches or even double two by fours with ten inches of insulation and an R value of 30. The cost of additional insulation would be far less than the cost of a replacement cooler. In the long run, it is better to keep your refrigeration needs down by using as much insulation as you can.

Regarding the seventy percent number, that must relate to peak times in summer. My homemade Arduino temperature monitor (detailed in my blog) showed my system running only around thirty percent of the time in April. In summer, it went up to sixty percent and I added some more refrigerant to bring it down to fifty. Now, it is winter again and my cooler is running fifteen percent of the time.

## Types

Four basic types of refrigeration systems are commonly in use.

## Window AC

Normal home window or through-the-wall air conditioners are not made for the temperatures usually encountered in a wine cellar, but there is a small overlap in their capabilities that allows their use. If you can be happy with your wine cellar running at sixty degrees instead of fifty-five, then you might be even happier with the extra thousand dollars in your pocket. Adding maximum insulation (R30 or more) to the cellar may allow temperatures a few degrees below sixty. Total replacement of the commonly available window unit will be cheaper than getting a technician to even open up your specialized wine cooler unit. And unless you live in a major city, your local technician is unlikely to have ever seen a unit like your wine cellar unit. That means repair cost will be even higher.

If a house AC is placed in a window, the condensate can be handled in the normal manner. If the wine cellar is in a basement, any condensate produced will have to be disposed of. Some people will be able to run a tube from the bottom of the back of the unit to a nearby floor drain. I have seen others install a bucket with a small pump and then run tubing overhead to the most convenient drain. Most likely, if your room is tight and you don't leave the door open, you may be able to live with a larger bucket and no pump. Note that most window units now have a mechanism for slinging the condensate into the condenser coil and evaporating it if the level gets too high.

### Self-Contained Wine Cooler

These are designed with wine cellar temperatures in mind and theoretically should be more reliable even down to temperatures of fifty degrees. Many comments on the internet contradict this theory, but I don't have any statistics. Condensate handling concerns are essentially the same as for the home window AC unit. However, the cost of those extra five or ten degrees will be five hundred dollars or more. For white wine, I don't question the need for a dedicated wine cooler system. For reds, I think it is questionable.

### Self-Contained Ducted Wine Cooler

These units are essentially similar to the units you would put through the wall but have stronger blowers to overcome the added resistance of the ductwork. The cooler can be put almost anywhere and ducts run to the wine cellar. This is similar to a home central AC where ducts are run to various rooms to provide air conditioning. The ducted cooler installation has to consider condensate handling and also comes with a high price.

**Split Units**

Built essentially like a house central air conditioning unit, these have an indoor unit and an outdoor unit connected by copper tubing and a control wire. A pan inside the unit collects condensate and it must be handled just as with the others.

*Wine Cooler Inside Unit*

For any units you are going to be installing yourself, make sure that the refrigerant used is R-134a. That way the refrigerant does not require any special permit and you may be able to do all the work on it yourself.

Some manufacturers provide for an external temperature sensor which they indicate you should put inside a bottle. I suspect that this type of control would allow greater temperature variations in the cellar by requiring the air temperature to vary more before the compressor is turned on. On the positive side, this may result in longer life of the compressor and fewer failures. Whether the temperature variation with this arrangement is excessive or not is unknown, but it appears unlikely.

In my unit, the temperature sensor which came with the unit was attached to the cooling coil with a plastic electrical tie. After the compressor shut off, the indicated temperature dropped by five degrees or more and did not warm up for ten minutes. Obviously, the sensor was measuring the coil temperature rather than the air temperature. I detached it from the cooling coil and stuck it a few inches out the intake grill and now the indicated temperature does not reflect the coil temperature.

**How it works**

The only reason I include this section is that the workings of refrigeration systems have been explained so poorly and even incorrectly in many of the manufacturers' web sites and also in some books. Having done design work on several refrigeration systems as large as sixty-thousand horsepower and at temperatures as low as minus two hundred forty degrees, I have a unique point of view that I hope will allow me to paint a clearer picture.

To begin with, most refrigeration systems in refrigerators, houses, cars, wine cellars and in chemical plants work by boiling a liquid. To boil a liquid requires heat. Just as in evaporating alcohol to make moonshine by boiling mash, it takes heat to turn a liquid into a vapor. (You didn't think I'd use some wimpy example like steaming broccoli, did you?)

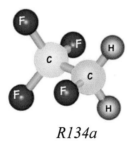

*R134a*

The molecule of R134a has two carbon atoms two hydrogen atoms and four fluorine atoms. (Note that I used F for fluorine, as Fl didn't fit well.)

The refrigerant in new car, house and wine cellar systems these days is (usually, but not always) R134a, a chemical which will boil at a relatively low pressure and temperature. As a historical note, R134a replaced R22 and R12 as these were believed to be depleting the ozone layer which protected us from UV rays from the sun. These refrigerants were believed to be causing, producing or enlarging a hole in the ozone layer. (Specifically, the hole is over Antarctica and the hundreds and possibly thousands of extra dollars we have each spent buying our AC units, refrigerators and car air conditioners over the last thirty years has resulted in only a few percentage point improvement in ozone and only slightly less sunburn for all Antarcticans. A major triumph for environmentalism.)

At any rate, environmentalism continues and R134a, although harmless to the ozone layer has been 'implicated' in global warming (or climate change or whatever) as a greenhouse gas. The EU has legislated that car AC's will no longer be allowed to contain R134a and another refrigerant must be used. The only currently viable replacement, according to Daimler Benz, produces toxic fumes when it burns, and is, therefore, hazardous in car fires. The EU is adamant that R134a has to go completely by 2017 and has to be gone in new models this year. (The new refrigerant is also only produced by one manufacturer and will be even more expensive.) So, it might be wise when you buy your cooler to buy a few extra cans of R134a from Wal-Mart and put them away in a nice cool dry place. (Maybe even in the wine cellar itself.)

A potential long-term replacement for R134a is carbon dioxide. A typical refrigeration cycle using carbon dioxide would have the low pressure side at over 400 psi and the high pressure side at 1200 psi or more. As much as I enjoy soldering, I would skip working on those systems. Sounds like it's soon going to be time for major insulation and solid state coolers, however expensive and inefficient they are.

# VAPOR PRESSURE
## R134a

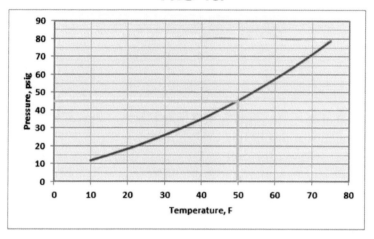

For refrigerant 134a, as it is used in cars and wine refrigeration systems, the boiler, or evaporator, operates at around 35 to 45 psi and 40 to 50 degrees F as shown by the vapor pressure chart above. That also means that no matter how long you run your cooler, or how well sealed your wine cellar will be, it will never cause the dew point to go below 50 degrees and most likely it will be five degrees higher. Thus, if there is minimal air flow through the wine cellar, there should also be minimal condensate to deal with after the cellar initially cools down.

# SPLIT UNIT LAYOUT

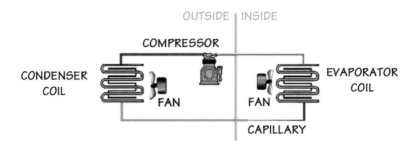

As shown in the Split Unit Layout above, the major components of a split unit are as follows:

The **evaporator coil** in the inside unit where a fan blows air through to evaporate the liquid refrigerant cooling the air and turning the refrigerant to a vapor.

The **compressor** in the outside unit that raises the pressure of the refrigerant so that it can be condensed at the temperature of the outside air.

The **condenser coil** in the outside unit where another fan blows air through the coil to condense the vapor refrigerant from the compressor at the higher pressure to a liquid. (This actually warms the outside air, which you can feel if you put your hand in the airflow exiting the outside unit. Thus, AC's are technically heat pumps.)

The **capillary tubing** (small tubing with a small inside diameter) which acts as a restriction between the high pressure in the condenser and the low pressure in the evaporator. In the capillary tubing, the refrigerant begins to boil, or flash, as the pressure reduces and the material entering the evaporator coil is actually a mix of vapor and liquid.

In most split AC units, one or two other parts are included. The **dryer**, which looks like a small soup can (or a moderate size automotive fuel filter) mounted just after the liquid leaves the outside unit, removes water from the system and prevents freeze ups in the capillary tube. The **sight glass**, which is adjacent to the drier, allows you to look for bubbles

52

in the liquid refrigerant, which would signal that you have lost some refrigerant through a leak. In many cars, the two are combined into a single cylindrical device under the hood.

For a single-unit type refrigeration unit, the four main elements are in one box and only one fan motor is used to turn the fans for both the evaporator coil and the condenser coil, otherwise everything is the same. Also, this is how your house and car air conditioners work and how your refrigerator works (unless you have a solid-state unit, which probably means you have a lot of money, and you can afford to hire someone else to build your wine cellar.)

A complication of this type of refrigeration system is the lubrication of the compressor. The oil used is actually mixed into the refrigerant, as you will see when you disconnect a refrigerant can from the system as you are filling it and your fingers become oily. Thus the vapor return line from the inside unit to the outside unit must avoid any low points to keep from having oil sitting in the pipe instead of sitting in the compressor.


## Temperature

The major question in this category is what is the best temperature to keep wine? The short answer is 55 to 62 for reds and 50 to 55 for whites. The authoritative answers I like the best are 'it varies' and 'nobody really knows.' The explanation of these is that, over time, wine undergoes many complex chemical reactions, many of which nobody understands.

Some of these tend to make wine taste better. Some, sadly, make wine taste worse. Some others tend to weaken the flavor. As in all cases of this kind, that means an optimum exists. It would be best to speed up the good reactions and slow down the bad ones, but that isn't possible. Generally, reaction rates drop by a factor of two for each ten-degree (Centigrade) drop in temperature, but that's just a round number. The number varies for each different chemical reaction. Some reactions actually increase at lower temperatures. The problem is that for each wine, for each type of wine, for each type of grape and for each combination of grapes, the optimum temperature is probably different. It is probably also different for each year of the wine's life and for each production year.

The wine cellars and caves deep beneath the surface stay at a temperature near the annual average for that area, no matter where the caverns are. The closer the cavern is to the surface, the closer it approaches the daily average. Soil a few feet below the surface will be at the daily average temperature. A few years ago, France had an unusually hot summer. Some of the cellars I toured had installed coolers. Many thought it was blasphemy.

The smart did what they believed they had to do and didn't worry about blasphemy. The cellars having problems were generally pretty close to the surface. The ceilings may have been only a few feet below the surface. The combination of all the stone and all the wine tended to keep the cellar at a temperature near the annual average, but the hot summer was just too much and temperatures climbed. Many wine makers bit the bullet and added air conditioning.

*Cote d'Or Vineyards*

The question becomes, is the proper temperature for French wines the temperature of French cellars or does the temperature in French cellars produce a wine we are used to and therefore that temperature is the best for producing the wine we are used to? The logic sounds a bit circular, but makes sense. However, maybe each wine matures at a different temperature and time peculiar to that wine. Also, does wine improve faster when it is young and more slowly when it is older? Then, does it reach a best point after which the flavor goes downhill. If so, wouldn't keeping older wines colder make sense? That would slow down all reactions, attempting to maintain flavor at its best point. So, in that case it would make sense to have a cellar with temperature zones. Maybe a few degrees warmer for younger wines and a few degrees colder for older wines. Is a few two or is a few ten?

The answer to all these questions is that nobody knows. Lots of theories, and few facts. No matter what the 'experts' think, they really don't know. How could anybody know how ten years at a particular temperature would affect any wine bottled this year? This year's wine is different from last year's wine. Admittedly, there is experience and opinion. The opinion of the best winemakers is probably better than the experience of all the rest. But, it is still a guess. And of course, wine makers are primarily concerned with making and selling the best wine they can rather than with determining the best conditions for storage.

It is easy to find charts which show which were good years for various wines. But these are all various people's opinions of wines. As an example, Burgundies were supposed to be bad in 2000, but I always liked those. They were more mellow. Drinkable earlier. And now thirteen years later, I still like them and they are even more mellow and still quite drinkable. I wish I had bought more. The experts said no. Who's right?

*Vineyards Along the Rhine*

I recently read an article that mentioned many horror stories regarding commercial storage of wine. Many commercial storehouses have no refrigeration at all and simply rely on the mass of the wine in the building to reduce temperature variation. Most of the wine stored in these places only stays for a short while, but some is stored for customers for many years. Another story told of someone who put a temperature recorder in a shipment that traveled several thousand miles. Temperatures over one hundred degrees F were recorded. The probability is that any wine you get will be treated better by you than by anyone else who has handled it.

At this point, it is reasonable to ask, "What's the bottom line?" Are the experts right or am I right? Maybe you are right. My answer is simply and finally that, if it's your money, then you are right. Weigh the facts, do what you think you should and don't look back.

The general belief regarding temperature is that cooler is better down to a point, then it's worse. Where that point is nobody knows. However, there is more agreement that consistency of temperature is more important than the temperature itself. So, whether you choose to keep your wine at fifty-five degrees or at sixty degrees or sixty-five, just stick to it - summer and winter. If you decide to decrease your cellar temperature as your collection ages, then do it. Neither you nor the experts will know the answer until the cork is popped and I'm not so sure about the experts.

From what I've read, I think that the failure of many cooling units results from the idea that wines should be stored as cool as possible. For red wines, a temperature of sixty to sixty-two degrees will keep your cooler working much better and much longer than if you try to maintain fifty-five degrees or less. A reasonable compromise is to have one or two small wine refrigerators to keep wines you want held at lower temperatures, say fifty to fifty-five degrees, and keep the rest at a more moderate temperature. These refrigerators, if small enough, could be kept inside the wine cellar.

*French Wine Barrel Storage*

A final minor point is that if you have a partial bottle left, don't put it into the refrigerator. That temperature is way too low. Put it somewhere in your wine cellar where the temperature will be right, not just for long-term storage, but also for short-term storage and drinking.

Regarding the best temperature for consuming wine, that is up to you as well. I prefer drinking the wine at cellar temperature or just bringing it straight from the cellar to the table. At one time, there were rumors about letting red wines warm to room temperature. I think that story came from France, but in France and much of Europe, rooms in winter were, and are now, considerably below temperatures most Americans keep their houses these days. So, forget what anybody else says and experiment.

## Humidity

In reading through the available literature, many people recommend a humidity of fifty to seventy percent in a wine cellar. I think these numbers are too high and a range of thirty to seventy percent is more reasonable. There are three problems with humidity. The first and probably most important is too much humidity. The second is somewhat minor and is too little humidity. The third is ignorance of humidity.

The first problem usually occurs when people build their cellar in the basement against a wall and use no vapor barrier and no insulation on those walls. Moisture comes through the walls and ruins wine labels. The simple answer is to build a wall of lumber and put in a vapor barrier, six-mil plastic preferred, on the outside along with insulation between the studs. Alternatively and better, build your walls a few feet from the basement wall and include a vapor barrier and insulation. The most common symptom of excess humidity is destruction of wine labels. Most people want to see what they are drinking and a moldy label gives a bad impression. If your wine labels mold over and you haven't noticed the high humidity, you aren't paying attention.

The second problem is not much of a problem so don't worry about it.

The third problem is solved if you get a hygrometer and read the previous two paragraphs. Hygrometers are readily available, electronic and manual.

The question of humidity is even less understood than the issues about temperature. Conventional wisdom says that a cork will dry out if it doesn't have enough humidity on the outside. But what about all that liquid on the inside? Isn't that enough to keep it moist? That's why we store wine horizontally. (Why some stores keep bottles vertical is another issue.) And then what about the seal or capsule which is put around the top of the bottle? I've been looking at those and I find it hard to believe that much of anything, air, moisture or humidity will migrate through.

In studying this issue, I ran across an article by Dr. Murli Dharmadhikari of Iowa State University which points out that when corks get excessively dry, they get crumbly. So, unless your corks get crumbly, you probably don't have a humidity problem or a cork age problem either. Also, in various places, I read that too much humidity is far worse than too little. A few percent more moisture inside the cork makes the cork susceptible to biological growth and that is extremely bad for your wine.

In an excellent book titled 'Wine Science: Principles and Applications,' the author, Ronald Jackson states, "Water loss from the cork in wine bottles is negligible." Due to aging and loss of elasticity, he comments that some people recork after 25 to 30 years. He also points out that bottles with wine leakage do not represent a risk of the wine going bad. The wine may be going out, but nothing else is going in. He also mentions that "Horace, the Roman poet, praises a wine aged for forty-six years." It was aged with a cork closure.

I have recently been drinking a number of 1997 to 1999 vintage wines. All the corks have been in good condition except those from one vintner. Those are crumbly, but not all of them. It appears that the issue of bad corks relates to the particular corks used and not so much to humidity. Most of the corks show a red inside end, occasionally extending a third of the way up the cork.

*Barrel Storage Requires High Humidity*

A number of articles recently published say that the need for high humidity in a home wine cellar is a myth. The myth began because wine stored in barrels does lose water, but not through a cork, through the barrel itself. Storing full wine barrels in a high humidity environment reduces the loss of water (and alcohol) through the barrel and increases the production of wine, sometimes as much as ten percent. Thus, construction of a wine cellar with high humidity for their barrels is a paying proposition for many wineries. (As a minor point, when touring wineries in Australia, they were proud that they had discovered the technique of making "unwooded" wines in stainless steel equipment, saying it was better than any wine from a barrel. Having lived in Saudi Arabia for a number of years, I am pretty sure the Aussies didn't invent the technique.)

The most logical answer I have heard and the one I believe is that humidity is more important to the people selling humidifiers than it is to the wine. One gentleman on the internet claimed that no matter how hard he tried and no matter how big his humidifier was, he couldn't get the humidity up to seventy percent and rarely over even fifty percent.

My cellar runs fifty percent in winter and seventy in summer. That's consistent with the humidity variations inside the house in those seasons.

I think the best answer is that if you think you should do something about humidity then consider one of two possibilities. First, humidify the air in your house. If it is not over thirty percent and preferably over forty percent in the winter, then you need to do something. The humans and the woodwork in your house will appreciate it far more than the wine. Second, if you are still concerned, add a small water feature to your cellar. They are pretty and they make a nice sound giving your cellar a nice ambience. That's another good reason to include some kind of counter as an architectural element. Also, make sure the counter has a handy electrical outlet.

## Noise

One would think that with the indoor unit only having a simple fan, noise from a split unit would never be a problem. However, if the inside unit is fastened solidly to a wall, the wall can become a sounding board and amplify the sound, many times. It is recommended that consideration for noise control be included in any design. One possibility is that, instead of mounting the unit tightly to the wall with the provided screw holes, a shelf should be provided and covered with two layers of carpet. The unit, split or self contained, can then sit on the carpet and transmit minimal noise.

The outside unit of a split unit can also have similar problems and the unit should not be placed near bedroom or dining room windows. If the final location ends up being noisy, the unit could be placed on rubber treads. It may also be useful to check for loose screws and tighten anything questionable. Noise control is an art and some trial and error may be required to find the best and lowest cost solution.

**Insulation**

In the early stages of planning, it is important to consider the type of wall construction and insulation to be used. The minimum wall thickness is around two and a half inches, made by using two by four lumber turned sideways. With drywall sheet used to cover the studs on inside and outside, that leaves one and a half inches for insulation between the studs. If fiberglass were used, that would provide an R value of around six, which is not much. If two by four stud walls were built normally, the R value for fiberglass would be thirteen or fifteen. To get more insulation, Styrofoam sheets can be screwed to the inside or outside and drywall screwed over that. A two-inch sheet of Styrofoam provides an R value of seven to ten. Recently, I checked the cost of insulation and R-30 bats were the cheapest insulation at one quarter to one eighth the price of solid foam. If you have the space, that seems the way to go.

As an alternate, sprayable polyurethane insulation is available on the internet and has a much higher R value per inch, around seven to eight. This would have an R value of as much as twenty-four in a two by four wall and would provide a vapor barrier at the same time. Unfortunately, the cost of spray foam is high, many times the cost of fiberglass insulation.

*Vineyard in Germany*
62

If space is available and you are doing your own construction, using two by six lumber would provide insulation of R-19 using fiberglass. Also, two walls using two by four lumber can be constructed, one inside the other, at three inches apart for a ten-inch stud cavity allowing an R value of thirty. That appears to be the most economical, well-insulated wall, if you have the space. Details of such an arrangement are shown later.

It is normal to install a vapor barrier to keep moisture from migrating from the warm side of the wall to the insulation and condensing there. If you use faced insulation, the facing provides adequate moisture resistance. Otherwise, or if you want to be thorough, six mil plastic sheeting is recommended. It is available at building supply stores in various widths and colors in large rolls.

## Electrical

Some years ago, one of the DIY channels had a program about people who had designed and built their own homes, all by themselves. Some of the people featured did all their own work and were quite inspiring. But, in most of these cases, the people did not really do all the work, but only most of it, which is still not bad. Some parts were contracted out.

But in virtually all cases, the electrical work was done by the homeowner. The reason the homeowner did not do all his own work was that some things, like building a foundation, were simply too strenuous for the average homeowner to tackle. All of the books I have read say "foundation building is a young man's game." I agree or at least it is a strong person's game and a game, like football, best played by a group. For all my house additions, I have contracted out the foundations. Some parts of house construction were judged too dangerous by many, like putting on roofs and shingles. But electrical materials are light and readily available. Tools required for electrical work are few and not expensive. It appears the perfect DIY subject. Thus, everybody featured on the show did their own electrical work and none had any misgivings.

In contrast, many of today's DIY shows appear to display two extremes only. Some people have no knowledge and no fear and end up making sparks and receiving a shock they will probably remember for the rest of their lives. Others believe that electricity is some demonic force which no normal human understands. I've watched as men just stared at the wires and women cried and yelled, "We need help."

In truth, electricity is not complicated and a few simple rules will keep you alive and spark free. That does not mean that the amateur should start tearing into the wiring in his house. But it does mean that if you read a book or two from your local building supply store, you will probably learn as much as you need to and avoid death or serious pain by electrons.

The electrical work required for a wine cellar amounts to providing wiring and an outlet for the air conditioning unit and wiring for the switches and lights. For installation into an existing room, the electrical equipment probably already exists and all that is needed is a healthy extension cord. If you build your own room, then running some wires and installing a few boxes is all that you need. It may be necessary to run a wire to your electrical panel and install a breaker, which are not difficult tasks, if you have a basement or crawl space. The work could be farmed out if necessary. For a split unit, a separate breaker, wiring and outside switch are required for the outside unit.

In my wine cellar, I used all LED lights to minimize heat, but lighting heat is minimal in all normal situations except the initial fill with bottles. I spread the fill over several days to make sure that the AC was not being overloaded. It is still a good idea to keep bottles a foot or so from incandescent lights. Fluorescent or LED lights have high efficiency and low wasted heat, which has to be removed with the AC. In this case, putting wine a few inches from a light fixture is acceptable. The amount of light provided can be varied by using different wattage bulbs in the various fixtures.

For planning purposes, one watt per square foot of floor space is a little dark, but maybe it provides some atmosphere. Two watts per square foot is good. Three watts is good enough to read wine labels. By using several fixtures, including ceiling cans, sconces and LED strips, the right light can be had wherever it is needed. The designer could plan to have three watts per square foot everywhere and then experiment with bulb sizes to get the right effects. Strip LED's are good for effects or to light a dark corner. Likewise, can lights can be had with directional eyeballs to point the light where it is needed. Regarding can lights, a rule of thumb is the can will illuminate a circle where the diameter of the circle is equal to the ceiling height of the room. So, with an eight-foot ceiling, a can will illuminate an eight-foot circle. Bulbs with different lighting patterns, such as wide pattern or narrow pattern, can be used to vary this rule of thumb.

# Chapter 4 - Design Details

In developing the final detailed design, it may be worthwhile to use a computer graphics program. The author has used AutoSketch (by the makers of AutoCAD) for many years and it is capable of making accurate and professional-looking drawings. It is a little more expensive than it once was, but is still quite affordable. Other programs exist and may even be a better buy, considering their price.

AutoSketch is adequate to do a wide variety of tasks without an excessively steep learning curve or an excessive first cost. Also, older versions may be available at a bargain price. If you already know a drawing program, then use it. If you have access to a discount price on a drawing program, then try it. Alternatively, using graph (cross section) paper and paper cutouts also works well if everything is done to a sufficient scale that the work is accurate.

In the end, putting tape on the floor and laying out the whole room on the floor should always be done whether you use a computer drawing program or paper and cutouts. The location of all studs, including AC supports and door king and jack studs, should also be shown. This helps greatly in laying out top and bottom plates when you start building the walls. Just lay them on the floor beside the tape and mark locations on the plates. After the studs and plates are drawn on the floor, then sketch in the wine racks and all other important features. Several times, a half hour of writing of the floor has uncovered a flaw in the design and saved me days of rework. Once the layout is on the floor, it is much easier to see exactly how it will all have to come together. The reason for using tape instead of writing directly on the floor is that if you have to make changes, you can strip off the tape and do it over. If you draw directly on the floor, making changes will be either difficult or confusing.

## Room Layouts

The following sketch shows an overall layout without concern for the type of racks for a wine cellar of about 2300 bottles.

## SQUARE ROOM
### 11 FT X 11 FT

**LENGTH OF RACK: 38 FT**
**2300 BOTTLES**

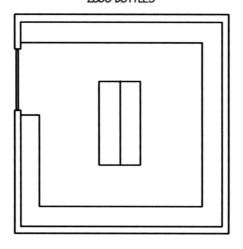

At first glance, it appears to have wasted space, not only in the corners, but also in the width of the passageways. One advantage is that there are several places where the AC unit could be placed and get reasonable air distribution without the use of auxiliary fans because there are no dead ends. Also, of course, it could hold more people than some layouts. To get the maximum number of bottles in this layout, the center section should extend all the way to the ceiling. However, the best appearance, and better air distribution would result from stopping the center racks at a counter or tabletop around waist high. This arrangement also suffers from being eleven feet across. The biggest ceiling span which can be used with two by four lumber (#2 Grade) is around nine feet. So, the ceiling joists would have to be two by six.

The next arrangement appears to reduce the wasted space, but doesn't actually work due to the efficiency of the wall-mounted racks extensively used in the first layout. In addition, the arrangement above provides the opportunity of placing a table top on the center racks without losing as much space as would be lost if the table top were placed on the center racks in the diagram below. The width of this layout is large enough that two by four ceiling joists are not sufficient without some kind of additional support. Two by six joists would be the minimum for a clear and simple ceiling.

## SQUARE ROOM
### 11 FT X 11 FT
### LENGTH OF RACK: 36 FT
### 2200 BOTTLES

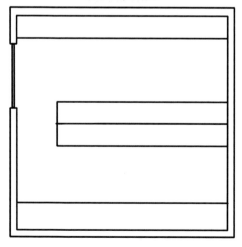

In the next arrangement, wasted space is reduced and room width is also reduced to the point where two by four ceiling joists are possible. The number of bottles remains the same. In both of these arrangements, the air conditioning airflow is blocked to part of the room unless the unit is placed just to the right of the door. A ceiling mounted fan blowing down the back corridor would probably be needed to overcome this drawback or the back section could be relegated to younger wines and they could be moved to the cooler front as they aged. (That sounds like too much work. Get a fan if your temperatures are off by more than a degree or two.)

# OFF SQUARE ROOM
## 11 FT X 9 FT
### LENGTH OF RACK: 36 FT
### 2200 BOTTLES

For a smaller layout, the design below was mentioned earlier. It will hold one thousand bottles and will accommodate magnum bottles as well as standard bottles in the corner racks. The end section could be made with a counter top with two feet of space, if desired. Also, an arch could be added there. The door shown is twenty-eight inches, a little small. A thirty-inch or thirty-six inch door could be allowed by increasing the room width by two or eight inches.

# 1000 BOTTLE LAYOUT

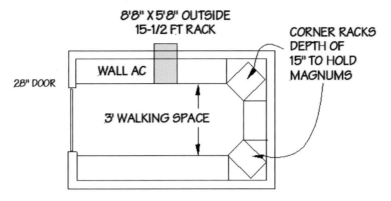

8'8" X 5'8" OUTSIDE
15-1/2 FT RACK

CORNER RACKS
DEPTH OF
15" TO HOLD
MAGNUMS

28" DOOR

WALL AC

3' WALKING SPACE

## Flooring

Wood flooring is desirable because it looks good and it is less likely for a dropped bottle to break. Trust me, I've tried it. Wood flooring is bad because a broken bottle will put a lot of liquid into the floor and will be virtually impossible to completely clean up. Getting water (or wine) into a wood floor is bad as it may cause deterioration of the floor. Replacing a single board in a hardwood floor is very difficult.

Different styles of wood flooring are available from three-quarter-inch thick solid oak and mahogany to engineered floors made like plywood with a one sixteenth inch thick surface layer. The engineered wood is more stable as the plies in the flooring are at right angles to each other, but can only be resanded once compared to as much as three times for solid wood strip flooring.

Laminated flooring is also available at a lower price than wood flooring. It is made of fiberboard with a picture of wood, or tile, on the top. (Oddly enough, ceramic tile is available which looks like wood.) Some varieties can be clicked together and a whole room snapped together in a few hours. The downside is that sometimes, tolerances are off and the click doesn't work right. Getting the piece back apart is difficult without marring adjacent pieces and usually wastes that piece. I installed this in a closet and a few pieces did not go together well. Also, of course, laminated flooring cannot be sanded. If it is damaged, repairing it is difficult. So, laminated flooring is not perfect, but it is easy and looks good.

Tile flooring is good because it is resistant to liquid, especially porcelain tile, but it is more likely to break a bottle. It can be installed in a wide variety of patterns and is available in a variety of sizes and colors.

Vinyl flooring over plywood underlayment is a good low-cost compromise and it can be had in tile as well as sheets in a variety of patterns, some mimicking the look of tile or wood. Concrete floors in basements may be cold in winter, but that may not be a problem unless it gets below fifty degrees in the basement. If so, add a plywood layer maybe over a one-inch layer of Styrofoam. Note that any wood should not be in direct contact with a concrete floor. Use a moisture barrier between the wood and the concrete. For holding shelving off the concrete floor, I have sometimes used a closed cell foam sold as a 'sill sealer'. However, it comes in large rolls and most would be wasted in a small job. Any kind of solid plastic or even a piece of vinyl tile would work well to keep racks off the concrete. It is best to have any piece of wood next to the floor be treated wood.

## Building the Room

For the wine cellar itself, there are many choices. The first is size. Determining the rough dimensions has already been discussed, but there are many details remaining.

**Bottle size** - The size of the bottles in my cellar is around one foot long by three and a quarter inches in diameter. However, the diameter of some is three and three-eighths. Half bottles are around two and a half inches and magnums are around four and one-eighth inches. Magnums are around fourteen inches long. For your cellar, it would be wise to measure the bottles you have and make sure the spacing is satisfactory. A margin of an extra quarter of an inch is fine for the bottles I have.

**Aisle size** - The interior aisles in the wine room should be at least two feet wide, but three feet gives a better impression. Four feet would be nice, and would make the end walls better for architectural elements.

**Wall thickness** - More insulation is almost always better, but the walls can still be made from two by four studs with sheets of polystyrene insulating board attached outside and/or inside with screws to provide more insulation. Then drywall sheets or other wall covering can be added over that. All of this should be included in the final drawings and on the final drawing made on the floor of the wine cellar.

**Door size** - Doors come in standard widths of 24, 28, 30, 32 and 36 inches and are generally 78 inches tall. If you are using an interior-type door, all these widths are available. For an exterior type door, only some are available. Before beginning construction, it is best to make the decision on the specific door you are going to use. If it is going to be purchased, then buy it before starting construction, if it is anything unusual or not normally stocked. If it is stocked at the store, then talk to the people there and learn the options available, including wall thickness for the wall into which the door fits. Interior doors are generally one and three-eighths inch thick and exterior doors one and three-quarters.

Doors can be purchased alone or pre-hung, with their hinges, jambs and one or two sets of facings already attached. The attached jambs are designed for a limited range of wall thicknesses. If you are building walls thicker than walls with two by four studs alone, then extension jambs may be required or you may have to construct them yourself. If you are making your own jambs, then just measure your wall thickness before cutting boards for the jambs. If the wall thickness varies, use the widest measurement.

Doors purchased separately from the jambs are available drilled or not drilled for handles and lock sets. If you get one which is not predrilled, jigs, with appropriate hole saws to make the required cuts, are available to simplify the process. Jigs are also available to help mount the hinges, some inexpensive and some at several hundred dollars. If I were only doing one door, I wouldn't buy the hinge jig.

*Wine Room Door*

Doors also have what is called hand. In other words, doors are left handed or right handed depending on which way it opens and whether it opens into the room or out into the hallway or basement. Before deciding to make the door open into the room, make sure you have adequate clearance for the door to swing. Clearance should allow for base moldings and face frames. By making the door open outwards, there may be a slight advantage in required air conditioning.

### Door facings

Doors require facings and jambs. The facings require about two and a half inches or more on each side of the door. Make sure you understand the size of your facings before finalizing your design, if you are tight on space.

### Wall covering

Drywall sheeting is commonly used, but many types of paneling are also available, including some appearing to be brick and stone, depending on the appearance desired and your budget. For high-end cellars, imitation rock is a good substitute for real stone as it does not require any foundation. Some types are made from plastic and are easy to install, but most are made from concrete and require some kind of cement to attach them to the wall.

### Moldings

Watching shows on TV where people are trying to sell their house, it is amazing that so many people are impressed by the look of crown molding. For painted moldings, moldings made of fiberboard, plastic foam and wood are available. These are easier to paint and cut at another location and then bring in and install in the cellar. For hardwood moldings, if you have a wood shop, you can make them yourself. Otherwise, they are expensive. A pneumatic nail gun capable of using two and a half inch nails is handy for installing crown moldings as well as base moldings.

## Refrigeration

Sites which sell air conditioning equipment for wine cellars tend to rate their equipment by the size of the cellar and finding the Btu capacity is sometimes difficult. Nonetheless, a simple treatment may be useful, especially for those with large cellars or unusual situations.

Heat leak into the wine cellar can be summarized in six categories: walls, ceiling, floor, doors, windows, and air infiltration. (Those weak of heart or easily bored can skip to the summary at the end of this section.)

For the first five categories, one equation does all the work.

$$Q = U A \triangle T$$

In this equation, Q is the amount of heat in Btus per hour to be moved, U is a heat transfer coefficient and delta T is the temperature difference across the wall. U can be considered a conductivity which is the inverse of the R value of the wall. Substituting in the R value, the equation becomes the following:

$$Q = \frac{A \triangle T}{R}$$

R is the resistance to heat transfer and is printed on the package of insulation. For two-by-four studs, most fiberglass bats have an R value of 13, although 15 can be found. Styrofoam has an R value of five per inch giving 17.5 if put between studs, but that would be difficult as it would have to be cut precisely. Spray foam is available on the internet and has an R value of around seven per inch or around 24 for a two-by-four stud cavity.

# 1000 BOTTLE LAYOUT

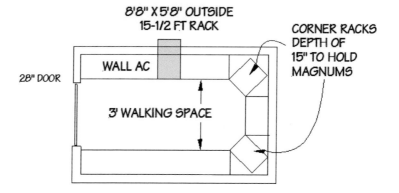

8'8" X 5'8" OUTSIDE
15-1/2 FT RACK

CORNER RACKS
DEPTH OF
15" TO HOLD
MAGNUMS

WALL AC

28" DOOR

3' WALKING SPACE

## Inside Walls

For an example used before, for an internal room in a one story house, the width is five foot eight (W = 5.67), length is eight foot eight (L = 8.67) with eight foot walls (H =8). Ignoring any windows or doors, the wall surface area:

A = 2 * W * H + 2 * L * H
A = 2 * 5.67 * 8 + 2 * 8.67 * 8
A = 90.3 + 138.7
A = 229 sq. ft.

Plugging this value into the equation and assuming a 70-degree temperature in the surrounding house and a 55-degree inside temperature and an R value of 13, we get:

Q = 229 * (70 - 55) / 13
Q = 264 Btu/hr. Not much.

For the ceiling, assuming an attic temperature of 140 in the summer and a ceiling R value of 30, which is minimum code, we get:

Q = 5.67 * 8.67 * (140 - 55) / 30
Q = 140 Btu/hr. Still not much.

For the floor, assuming a crawl space with a temperature of 85 and a floor R value of 19, again minimum code, we get:

Q = 5.67 * 8.67 * (85 - 55) / 19
Q = 78 Btu/hr. Not much.

The total heat loss for the room through walls, ceiling and floor is then as follows:
Q = 229 + 264 + 140
Q = 633 Btu/hr. Again not much.

## Outside Walls
So, why are AC units rated for much higher cooling loads? Possibly because few wine cellars are totally contained inside the first floor of a house. It would be normal to use an existing bedroom as a wine cellar. If so, then one wall could be an outside wall. How does this affect things?

For an inside wall:
Q = 8.67 * 8 * (70 - 55) / 13
Q = 80 Btu/hr.

For an outside wall:
Q = 8.67 * 8 * (95 -55) / 13
Q = 213 Btu/hr.

This is an increase in 133 Btu/hr. raising the total to 746 Btu/hr.

## Air Infiltration
Air Infiltration is a major source of heat loss for most houses. For a typical older house, air infiltration is generally measured at around one and a half house volumes per hour. That is extremely hard to believe, but it has been measured many times. Newer and better-built houses have infiltration rates of down to one half a house volume per hour. One would presume that a wine cellar would have rates closer to the low end as only one entrance exists and usually no windows. Also, the number of wall penetrations is low with only one light switch and maybe only one power outlet and a ceiling light. Making the space beneath the door as small as possible is a

good idea and putting foam tape on the doorstops will also help decrease air infiltration.

First to be calculated is the volume of the room.

$$V = L\ W\ H$$

V = 8.67 * 5.67 * 8
V = 393 cu. ft.

Next the amount of air moving through the room.

$$m = \rho\ V$$

The Greek letter rho stands for the density of air or 0.74 pounds per cubic foot.

m = 0.074 * 393
m = 29 pounds.

So for an air infiltration rate of one-half volume per hour, that would be 14.5 pounds of air exchanged with the house per hour. The cooling requirement is the amount of heat necessary to cool this air down to room temperature. The heat capacity of air is 0.24 Btu/lb./deg F. The temperature difference is the temperature of the attic or around 140 degrees minus the wine cellar temperature or around 55 as a worst case.

$$Q = m\ C\ \Delta T$$

Q = 14.5 * 0.24 * (140 - 55)
Q = 296 Btu/hr.

This is 296 Btu/hr. lost through air infiltration from the attic. Relative to the other numbers, it is significant. If the air being brought in were coming in from the house in the summer, this number would be only 52 Btu/hr. or one sixth the value of bringing air in through the attic. Thus, make sure any ceiling penetrations and light fixtures and cans are well caulked. The admonition to use airtight cans is well founded. Also, note that the cans should be caulked around the penetration in the drywall. If a fixture is used over a ceiling electrical box, the fixture should also be caulked to the ceiling along with filling any open screw holes with caulk.

## Doors and Windows

What about the effect of a door? For this calculation, I will assume a thirty-six inch wide door, seventy-eight inches tall. As wood has an R-value of one per inch, an indoor rated solid wood door would, at best, have an R of one and a half. The door used for the front door when I moved to my current house was indeed solid wood, but the panels were only about a half an inch thick. It's R-value could not have been greater than one. Plus, it was warped and leaked around the edges.

On the other hand, indoor solid wood slab doors are not sold, but have some kind of particleboard interior. In cutting through such a door, the interior is not solid like particleboard, but less dense. Some sources suggest that some types of manufactured board have R values as high as 2.4 per inch. That would provide a door with an R value of around 3.

I have also cut through many hollow core doors. They are mostly air with a small amount of foam for spacers. A clever person could cut a number of quarter-inch holes in such a door and put in some minimally expanding spray foam to greatly improve the R-value. But without such modifications, I would assume an R-value of around 2. With the foam, you might get up to five or six.

The only authoritative information I could find was from Pella and they claim their solid doors (I couldn't tell which of their many doors this was.) had an R-value of 7. That would seem to be an extremely high number as Styrofoam only has an R-value of 5 per inch. In fairness, other types of foam do have R-values of around 7 per inch. So, the Pella number is defensible.

I will do the calculations for two doors, one with an R value of 2 and one of 7.

Heat loss through similar size wall space:
A = 36 * 78/ 144
A = 19.5 sq. ft.

Q = A dT/R
Q = 19.5 * (70 - 55) / 13
Q = 23 Btu/hr.

For the low R value (2) door, we get:
Q = 19.5 * (70 - 55) / 2
Q = 146 Btu/hr.
Or a net increase of 123 Btu/hr.

For the high R value (7) door, we get:
Q =19.5 * (70 - 55) / 7
Q = 42 Btu/hr.
Or a net increase of 19 Btu/hr.

I have seen many admonitions regarding not putting glass doors in wine cellars, but double-pane windows have an R value of two and triple pane windows have an R value of three. (Pella claims some windows of ratings up to 5.) Thus, they would be no worse than a hollow core or solid interior door. Also, a single pane window would have an R value of one and would add another hundred Btus/hr. or so.

The calculation for a window, which might exist in an existing room is similar and if the window had an area of one third of the area of the door calculated, then its contribution could be another 100 Btu/hr. Note that older double-hung windows may leak considerably.

Finally, as mentioned, some of the best wine cellars I have seen are part of the dining room and have one wall of half-inch thick glass. As long as the dining room is air conditioned, the cost in cooling is not great. However, the ambience is amazing.

## Summary

Calculation summary.
Interior walls      264 (4 walls)
One exterior wall 133 extra
Ceiling             140
Floor               78
Door                19 to 123
Window              100
Air infiltration    52 to 296
Total               786 to 1134 Btu/hr.

Thus, for this design, the total AC requirement is less than to a little above 1000 Btu/hr. If AC units are running much of the time, then something must be wrong. Possibilities include, a far bigger room than planned, no or little insulation in the walls, ceiling or floor, insufficient ventilation in the attic, excessive air infiltration from outside or especially from the attic or leaving the door open too much.

A great many existing houses are not up to code on attic insulation or floor insulation. Also, existing interior walls are not generally insulated. Most electrical boxes in most of the country are not sealed and many lighting cans are neither sealed nor insulated. All these things contribute to heat loss.

Obviously, some of these are easy to fix, like keeping the door closed or putting weather stripping around the door. If a window is leaking, taping the gaps can help. Also, putting a sheet or two of polystyrene or polyurethane insulation over a window is a good idea. It decreases heat loss as well as reducing light. The insulation in the attic is easy to supplement and R-30 bats are cheap and easy to install (but not in the summer or on a sunny afternoon). A high efficiency air mask is a good idea any time you are in the attic. If the house has a crawl space, increasing insulation under the floor to R-19 is also relatively easy in most cases.

# Chapter 5 - Wine Cellar Construction

## Building the Room

The simplest and least expensive option for obtaining the space for a wine cellar (not to beat a dead horse) in an existing house is to convert an existing room. In this way, no walls have to be built, no floor has to be covered and no ceiling has to be constructed. Likewise, a window is usually available to hang a small, 5000 Btu per hour, window air conditioner. An analog air conditioner is preferred as units with digital controls tend to shut themselves off during a power failure or even a short blip and do not restart themselves. If you check your wine cellar every day and always consult your thermometer, then that problem may not be major. Larger units are difficult to find with analog controls (but many larger, hotel-style AC units do have analog controls).

If an existing room is not available for conversion, several alternatives are available. The simplest option may be to build a dedicated room in the basement. Using existing outside uninsulated walls is questionable as they are likely to be too hot in the summer, too cold in the winter and possibly too damp. Adding a moisture barrier, a two by four stud wall and insulation is still recommended on outside walls as the wall is unlikely to stay at the correct temperature year around and concrete walls are almost impossible to cool down or heat up.

The building code says that for ceilings up to nine feet wide a two by four, No. 2 grade (not stud grade) ceiling joist is adequate. That should be good enough for most smaller wine cellars. Walls in basements should be covered with six mil plastic on the warm side, outside of the wine cellar, before putting up studs, to avoid excessive humidity condensing inside the insulation (according to theory). If putting the cellar against a basement wall, six mil plastic should be attached to the wall first or the studs first before putting the wall in place. Leaving a two-foot inspection space between the wall and the wine cellar would be good practice where space is available. Spray foam is available on the internet for use by us amateurs, but is much more expensive than fiberglass bats. Full body protection should be worn when spraying including a head covering and non-vented goggles for the eyes.

*Foam and Fiberglass Insulation*

The picture above shows three different installation types for insulation. The blue Styrofoam was used around a pocket door where the two by fours were turned sideways and only one and a half inches was available on each side of the pocket. The paper-faced R-19 fiberglass was used for the rest of the walls. For the ceiling, two R-30 bats were used with the top layer perpendicular to the bottom and with a six-mil poly vapor barrier on the bottom. In the center, lower part of the picture, a blue electrical box can be seen protruding out from the insulation where the front side will be even with the drywall installed next.

A good book on house construction should be consulted if you want to build a room in the basement or add a wall to an existing room and you don't have that experience. The following discussion mentions the high points and is not intended to be all-inclusive.

## Walls

The basic components of most walls are two by lumber, insulation, and drywall sheets, all held together with screws and nails. The lumber is assembled as shown in the following diagram although there are many variations. For most walls in the warmer states, two by four lumber is used for house construction. It will support R-13 fiberglass insulation.

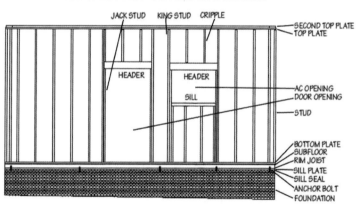

TYPICAL WALL LAYOUT FOR NEW CONSTRUCTION

Insulation of R-15 can be found at a somewhat higher price to fit inside two by four walls. (Note that a two by four is actually one and a half inches thick by three and a half inches wide. A two by six is five and a half inches wide. A two by eight is seven and a quarter inches wide. Apparently, it has something to do with planing down rough lumber of the original thickness, but I've planed too much wood to believe that.)

Thicker walls can be built to provide more insulation or better insulation and I recommend it. Spray foam is available on the internet for DIY use. It will provide R-values well over twenty for a two by four framed wall, but the cost is many times that of fiberglass, as mentioned before.

This type of construction may work in a basement where the ceiling is obstructed and the walls are built shorter than the room height. Generally, walls are assembled with the wood lying on the floor. Two sixteen-penny nails are driven into each end of the studs through the top and bottom plates, headers are attached with nails and then the whole assembly is tilted into place. However, if one tries to tilt an eight foot wall into an eight foot space, it won't fit as shown in the exaggerated sketch below. Although this is a simple concept, I have watched numerous DIY shows where they forget about it. Grown men screamed and women cried.

**TILTING A WALL
INTO PLACE**

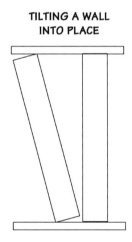

An easy alternate is to use two bottom plates. The first bottom plate is attached to the floor and then the wall, now one and a half inches shorter, can easily be tilted into the vertical and lifted into place on top of the second bottom plate. (Having to pound the wall into its final position with a hammer is often considered a measure of a good wall, rather than an indication of a mistake. I believe it, anyway.)

TYPICAL WALL LAYOUT FOR BASEMENT CONSTRUCTION

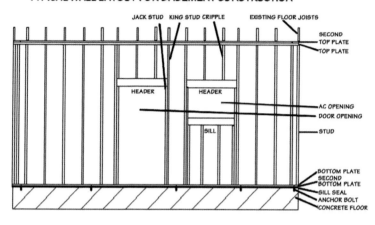

Note that if the wall is erected on a concrete floor, the bottom plate in contact with the floor should be made of treated wood and a moisture barrier provided between the concrete and the wood. The bottom plate is then fastened to the floor with screws or nails before the wall is erected. If two bottom plates are used, the screws are attached in shallow cutouts deep enough to keep the screw heads from interfering with the upper bottom plate. Also, in a basement installation where the walls are not actually load-bearing, the second top plate is optional. If the second top plate is omitted, attach the sidewall to the end wall at the top with a Simpson Strong-Tie or equal steel strap. The strap can be placed over the top or around the side of the top plates.

A second alternate is to install top and bottom plates first then install each stud, measuring them all individually and toenailing them into place with four eight-penny nails at each end. The top plate can be temporarily set in place by nailing or screwing to the floor joists above. This is a great application for the laser tape measure listed in the Appendix. Just shoot the distance, cut the stud a hairsbreadth long and hammer and nail it into place.

Note that many of the television DIY shows are made in Canada and the codes are different there. If the room must meet code, then nails should be used as the required fasteners. Part of the reason screws are not accepted by the code is that the US does not have standards for screws and many tons of drywall screws are readily available. Drywall screws are made from a brittle grade of steel and they easily break, intentionally. If you use screws for any attachment other than sheet rock, use a higher grade of screws such as construction screws. Also, for nails or screws going into treated wood, they should be hot-dip galvanized.

Once the walls are installed, the bottom plates crossing the door opening are usually cut out with a reciprocating saw or an oscillating saw. Don't forget that the opening for a thirty-six inch door is not thirty-six inches wide But thirty-eight inched because space has to be provided for a three-quarter inch doorjamb on each side plus some space for shims to plumb the door. Also, framing is rarely perfectly straight, so allow for a little variation in angles and widths. An opening of at least two inches wider than the door and one inch taller than the door is recommended. If you use a doorsill or a pre-hung outdoor type door with a sill, measure the whole assembly first to make sure you have allowed enough height in your rough-in opening.

After the walls are in place and the sections are nailed together, electrical wiring is put in place. Again, there are many good books about wiring and one should be read before attempting electrical work for the first time. In general, small plastic or metal boxes are attached to the studs to house connections for switches and light fixtures. All connections between wires should be made inside a box, which will be accessible after the construction is finished. It is acceptable to install a box, which only has connections and no switches, outlets or fixtures. This is done if you have an existing wire and it is not long enough. Just put in another box and make the connection with wire nuts inside the box. Put a blank plate over it after the drywall is in and make sure the plate is accessible after all the racks are installed. The DIY shows on TV show endless examples of wires being spliced inside walls or ceilings and then covered over. If these should some day work their way loose, a fire could result.

The wires between boxes should go through holes in studs. The holes should be a minimum size (three-quarters of an inch works for two cables), centered in the stud and are best drilled before assembling the walls. So, don't wait for the walls to be finished before deciding where your outlets, switches and lights should be placed. Put them into your original plan before the first nail is driven and draw them onto the plan you draw on the floor before starting construction. That way you will know which studs need holes and which do not. Alternatively, put a hole in every stud about three feet above the bottom.

After the wiring is installed, insulation is added. The easiest to use insulation is paper-faced fiberglass bats with the paper facing placed on the warm side, which is the outside of the wine cellar. I have seen at least one map, which shows that houses in many parts of the country from the mid-Atlantic region west don't really need to have a moisture barrier. Also, I have read that three coats of paint is an excellent moisture barrier. On the other hand, conventional wisdom says to use 6 mil plastic sheet if you use unfaced bats. The paper-faced bats are easier to install as the paper can be stapled to the studs, supporting the bats. Otherwise, the bats are a friction fit and a little out of tolerance in the sixteen-inch (center to center) stud spacing will allow the bat to slip.

According to the simplified psychrometric chart on the next page, following the red line, if your indoor temperature is 75 degrees F or above and your relative humidity is 50 percent or above, then you have to cool the wine cellar walls down to 55 degrees before you will get any condensation inside the wall. If your wine cellar were kept at 60 degrees, then you would not have any concern about condensation under these conditions. If your relative humidity were 30 percent, instead, you would have to cool your wine cellar down to forty degrees to produce condensation. Not likely.

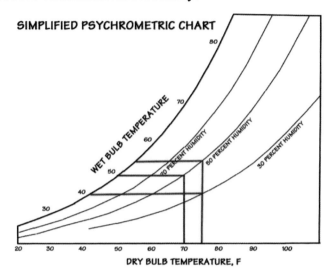

At temperatures above 75 and humidity above 50 percent, condensation on the inside wall of the wine cellar is theoretically a problem. As shown by the blue line, at a house temperature of 70 and 30 percent humidity, your wine cellar would have to be below fifty to have condensation.

So, for an inside wine cellar at sixty degrees, as long as the house temperature is below 75 and humidity below 50 percent, the moisture barrier is not an issue.

The whole issue of humidity control gets far more confused if we look at summertime conditions. In most climates, the vapor barrier on houses is placed on the inside as wintertime conditions are a concern. But if we have a day where the outside temperature is 100 degrees with fifty percent humidity, then an inside temperature of 75 would cause condensation inside the insulation. And yet, this does not seem to be a problem. I have taken apart walls where conditions like these have existed and have seen no signs of water or mold. Likewise, I have worked on ceilings where these conditions have existed with no sign of water of mold. The DIY shows on TV seem to only find mold where liquid water has seeped in or where air could blow through the wall. Both of these should be avoided like the plague in your wine cellar.

The bottom line is that, if you can install six-mil plastic on the warm side of your walls, then do it. If you can't install a vapor barrier on the warm side, some say to put it on the cold side. In any event, I would recommend putting drywall mud and tape on all joints and primer with at least one topcoat on all walls. An extra coat of either primer of topcoat would be desirable.

As mentioned in the beginning of this section, the third main component of walls is the wall covering or in most cases gypsum board, also called sheet rock, wallboard and drywall. For simplicity, the latter name will be used. Drywall comes in four-by-eight and four-by-twelve-foot sheets, generally half an inch thick. The sheets have beveled edges on the two long sides to enable joints between sheets to be covered with tape and mud without any bump in the wall. The tape provides reinforcement to the joint to avoid cracks.

For walls longer than eight feet, many people use the twelve foot length installed horizontally as there are fewer mud joints. At the same time, a sheet of drywall is brittle, heavy and cumbersome. I use the eight-foot length and often install it vertically. The drywall is installed with large-head nails or with special drywall screws. The screws are made of brittle steel so that the heads can break off if they are driven too hard or too far. So, if you have any of these screws left over, don't use them anywhere you need a strong attachment. The normal screw length is one and a quarter inches but longer screws are available if you installed a layer of polystyrene over the studs to have better insulation. Coarse thread screws are used for wood framing and fine thread screws for metal framing.

Drywall nails are driven with a hammer and the technique involves dimpling or pounding the nail just hard enough to get the head to go just slightly below the surface. The depression is then filled in with drywall mud. Similarly, drywall screws can be driven with a conventional drill and a phillips head bit to just below the surface. Special drywall screwdrivers and screwdriver bits are available which disengage the bit just as it breaks below the surface. For me, the devices seldom work as advertised and a simple phillips bit with a variable speed cordless drill works fine.

Drywall mud is available premixed in gallon buckets or five-gallon buckets as well as in powder form. The five-gallon buckets are only slightly more expensive than the one-gallon buckets and you get a heavy-duty, handy five-gallon bucket for free. Also, drywall mud can be purchased as a dry powder and mixed on site. In this case, mud can be purchased which sets up more quickly than the premixed variety allowing several coats to be applied in one day. Because the mud shrinks when it dries, three coats are often needed. I'm not good at mudding and I frequently need four or five coats to get a flat wall.

The mud available in buckets may require most of the day for a one-eighth inch thick layer to dry. For thicker layers, overnight is necessary. The mud is spread on the surface of the drywall using a flat-bladed 'knife' to fill in any marks or nail or screw holes and to fill in between sheets covering the drywall tape. Knives are made in various quality grades from steel, stainless steel and plastic and in various widths. As a minimum, a six-inch knife and a two-inch knife are useful. A ten-inch knife is also good for long edge joints.

The corner detail in the following page shows a number of other features of wall construction. The spacing of the studs is normally 16 inches and that works well with 48-inch drywall or decorative paneling.

Ending the sheets over a stud makes the joint less likely to crack. In this layout, where sheet goods are used both inside and outside the wall, the studs should be placed so that the outside sheets end over a stud as it is probably the most visible.

# CORNER DETAIL
## TOP VIEW

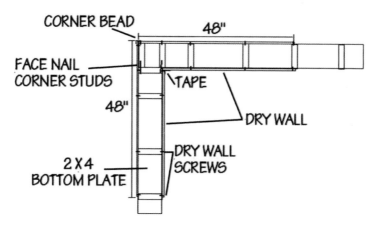

The inside sheet at the corner cannot end at a stud because of the corner geometry. Thus, the inside sheets must be cut, or snapped. Cutting the sheets in the corner will make the cut less noticeable as the beveled side of the cut sheet will be over a stud and can be taped and mudded easily to the next sheet. Also, it is likely that a rack will cover the corner and disguise any bad inside mud joints. Drywall isn't actually cut, but the paper facing is cut with a razor knife and the cut line is snapped. The paper facing on the opposite side is then cut with a razor knife.

The outside corners are usually covered with a corner bead. These are made from metal or plastic and attached with drywall nails or screws or even spray glue. If you have gone totally crazy with your architecture, corner beads are available with cuts in the flanges for use around curves. For outside corners other than ninety degrees, a corner bead is available in a roll and uses paper and metal and can be bent to any angle. (That type of corner bead is usually attached with drywall mud as glue. Use plenty and then squeeze the excess out with a drywall knife, then cover with more mud.) The purpose of the corner bead is to protect the corner from someone or something bumping into it and making a dent. Also, use of a corner bead makes the corner look sharper and neater. After being nailed or screwed in place, the corner bead is coated with mud to smooth over the flanges and nails or screws.

All drywall joints between sheets are taped and mudded, including the joints between walls and ceiling. This helps make the whole room air tight with minimal air infiltration. It is also a good idea to caulk the bottom of the drywall to the subfloor and then caulk all joints in the subfloor to minimize air infiltration. Fiberglass tape is easier to use than paper tape but some sources say it's only half as strong. If you have any reason to suspect a joint might move, two layers of fiberglass tape can be used, offsetting each a bit. The fiberglass tape comes with an adhesive that makes it easy to stick to the joint. The adhesive is not terribly sticky and it is necessary to be careful to not pull the tape off while applying the first layer of drywall mud.

Getting enough mud onto the paper tape without it drying out has always been a problem for me. I have had to rebuild a number of taped joints. Professionals use a gadget ($90) containing a box of mud where the paper tape is pulled through the box to cover and saturate it with mud. I have never wanted to part with that much money for something so little used. In retrospect it would probably have been worth it, if I had gotten one ten years ago. (I recently saw one made of plastic on TV for less than $50.)

Placing drywall on a ceiling is more difficult than on walls as the sheet must be supported on both ends while being screwed in several places. Having two friends help you, or a friend and a wife, will make the job much easier. I have seen a man and his wife alone do it on TV and it is not for the faint of heart or weak of knees. It is better to rent a drywall lift from a local rental outlet. The sheet is placed on the lift and cranked up into place. One person alone can then put in the screws.

When we built the eleven-foot barrel ceiling in the living room, the commercial drywall lifts were not tall enough and I ended up making my own from two by fours, rollers and a cheap manual winch from Harbor Freight. With rental fees around thirty dollars per day, it was well worth the money. My wife referred to it as the 'death machine' and refused to go near it, but it never showed any outward signs of malevolence.

The curved sections of drywall in the barrel ceiling benefitted from a T-shaped support made from a two by four and a piece of plywood on the end cut to the curvature of the ceiling. We would push it against the center of the sheet and push until the drywall hit the curved ceiling joists, then jam it into the floor to hold it while enough screws were installed to keep in in place. Then the death machine was removed and the remainder of the screws could be installed from a ladder.

*Box for Electrical Outlet*

As shown in the picture above, electrical boxes are usually installed sticking out from the stud by half an inch to be flush with the outside of the drywall after it is installed. In this case, also note that the two by six corner configuration allows surfaces for attachment of drywall. The pocket behind the corner was stuffed with fiberglass insulation before the outer sheathing was attached and the hole where the wire penetrated the corner studs was caulked to minimize air infiltration.

Wires are installed before the insulation or the drywall is installed and all wires are tucked back inside the box. As the drywall is being installed, holes are cut in it to allow the electrical boxes to stick through. This can be done after the first few screws are installed using a spiral saw or before installing the drywall by using a keyhole saw and careful measurements. My wife bought my keyhole saw many years ago at a yard sale for a dollar. It has a pointed blade, bent in many places by mistake, and when the handle broke, I glued it back together. But, it still works. Most of the time I use the spiral saw, but it is easy for things to go wrong with the spiral saw and it makes a lot of fine dust. (By the way, keep the drywall and drywall mud dust off your skin, especially your scalp. I think that led to my allergy to hair dye.)

As a variation on the layout shown previously, consider using superinsulation, of R-30, or better instead. In the following layout, R-19 bats can be installed between studs from both sides giving an overall heat resistance of R-38. If the studs in the two walls were aligned, then R-30 bats would be much cheaper and almost as good. For a room as small as a wine cellar, and with high AC equipment costs, the extra insulation should result in a longer life for your cooler as well as lower electricity cost and of course a more uniform temperature in the wine cellar.

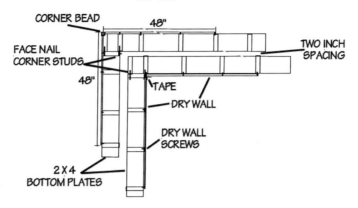

## CORNER DETAIL
## W/R30 SUPERINSULATION
### TOP VIEW

CORNER BEAD

48"

FACE NAIL
CORNER STUDS

TWO INCH
SPACING

48"

TAPE

DRY WALL

DRY WALL
SCREWS

2 X 4
BOTTOM PLATES

## Wall Finishes

A trip to the local building supply store will give you some good ideas about wall finishes. What you choose, like everything, is a matter of taste, cost, skill and time.

**Paint** - Drywall is easy to paint using a brush to cut in corners and a roller on the major surfaces. After the mud has cured and has been sanded and is flat without needing another coat, it should be primed using a primer intended for drywall, then given one or two top coats. Some people use two coats of primer to make sure the mud joints look the same as the drywall itself. Mud joints behind the racks, however, should be no problem. Two top coats are better if you don't use two primer coats as it provides a better moisture barrier. The final top coat can even have a faux finish, in areas where it is visible, and a great many are available. One thing to remember is that repainting the walls after the racks are installed is practically impossible. Think of that extra coat of paint as insurance. Five years later, you'll be happy you did it.

The major reason people use some kind of texture on the ceiling is that their mud job is not that good. I prefer putting on another coat of mud if the primer shows that the mud is not flat. Drywall mud will stick to primer without a problem. In fact, if you end up sanding through the paper surface of the drywall, some recommend priming the exposed gypsum before continuing with more mud.

If you do decide to texture the ceiling, various brushes and mops are available to help create a nice texture. From watching the DIY shows on TV, it appears that the old popcorn style of sprayed-on ceiling texture is out of fashion. Note that after texturing, the ceiling should be painted.

**Wallpaper** - We have applied wallpaper before and the textured types are particularly interesting. Some can be painted. I worry that in the humidity of the wine cellar, seams will open and after a few years, the wallpaper will look bad. Replacing the wallpaper in the cellar might be difficult. So, a more permanent solution is recommended.

**Tile** - A great variety of wall tile is available and it is even possible to get custom wall tile made from your own pictures. Also available are hand-painted tile made for a variety of settings and for wine cellars in particular. Tile is usually applied to walls using a mastic adhesive and a v-notch trowel. However, some heavier varieties use thin set cement and a square notch trowel. Tiles vary in price, from the inexpensive at one to three dollars per square foot to the more expensive tiles at fifteen to twenty dollars per square foot and even more for some unusual, hand-made or custom tiles.

**Stone** - Synthetic stone looks great and is readily available on the internet and at building supply stores in a variety of materials. The stone made from concrete is around one inch thick and comes in single pieces, blocks of half a dozen pieces and larger blocks attached to a plywood backing. None of those require any special structural work. Also available are four-foot-wide panels made from polyurethane and patterned to look like stone. Any of these would be great for select architectural features.

*Stone Appearance Paneling*

**Brick** - For my wine cellar, we chose a synthetic brick sheet product about a quarter of an inch thick for all the wall surfaces -- after pricing veneer brick. It is similar to paneling and looks a lot like brick. Other products are available including thin brick pieces that can be glued to the wall. For the areas behind the racks, real bricks or brick pieces are overkill. For select areas, it does look good.

**Wood Paneling** - Wood in exotic species looks great and costs no more than nicer tile. Mahogany veneered plywood costs less than $100 per sheet (2013) or a little over $3 per square foot. Solid wood mahogany costs around $5 per square foot. Again, putting this behind racks would be a waste, although using the cheaper grades of paneling made from fiberboard would be an easy way to cover over a bad mud job.

## Ceiling

The major consideration for the ceiling, as mentioned before, is the size of the rafters. Use of two by four lumber is consistent with the code up to nine feet in length. In that case, R-13 insulation could be put between the rafters and more could be put perpendicular, across the rafters if space is available.

*Fiberglass Attic Insulation Over Cellulose*

For a wine cellar in the top floor, the insulation in the attic above can easily be improved by adding bats of fiberglass perpendicular to the joists.

Note that, unlike the picture, bats should be pushed close together with no space between. (When you go to the building supply store to get lumber, two by fours are available not only in eight and ten foot lengths, but also in stud grade and number two grade with stud grade being cheaper and frequently more bent. I usually use number two for everything as it is usually better quality, straighter and only costs a dollar more. Usually.)

If the wine cellar is in the basement and the ceiling is up against the floor joists, then the maximum insulation is the depth of the floor joists for the floor above. Putting in the maximum insulation is a decision you only regret once, when you are standing in front of the cashier at the store. Extra insulation will make your expensive refrigeration system last longer and will pay for itself.

## CEILING JOIST LAYOUT

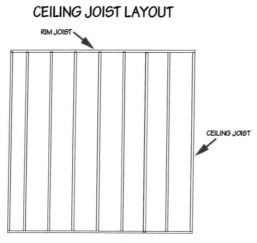

*Top View of Ceiling Joists*

Where new ceiling rafters are being installed in a basement, it would simplify their addition to add a rim joist along two sides of the ceiling just above the outer edge of the top plates. The rim joist is then face nailed into each ceiling rafter and that is what keeps the rafters vertical. The rafters and rim joist are also toenailed into the top plate. This also helps keep insulation in place.

## Door

Several choices are available for the door to your wine room, some commercially available and some DIY. Commercial doors come as hollow core inside doors, solid core wooden slab doors and rail and stile doors, as well as several styles normally sold as house front doors including wooden panel doors, metal covered doors and fiberglass doors. The refrigeration section of Chapter 4 pointed out the refrigeration cost of a poor door. If you can afford that cost, then you can get any door you like. Most of the wine cellar cooler manufacturers recommend against windows in doors, however, a window will have no worse heat loss than the poorest door calculated. Also, as mentioned before, some cellar builders advertise a whole wall of glass to separate the wine cellar from the dining room. I thought the look of a glass wall was way over the top and definitely makes an impression on your guests.

Although I made the heat transfer calculations, I think the door calculations are conservative. I couldn't find actual R values for many doors, and there is some experience to consider. I kept a temporary wine cellar with a wooden hollow door for seven years with no condensation on the door and no deterioration of the door. I did keep the cellar at sixty degrees, which I think is fine for reds and short term for whites.

Regarding DIY doors, it is possible to make a door from scratch and I have done that. It took a long time to make doors I was confident would not warp and over the last few years they have not. Those in the picture are between the entrance foyer and the formal dining room.

*DIY Pocket Doors*

Basically, to avoid warping, I made strips of plywood, turned them ninety degrees and glued them together, making homemade glulam boards. I then half-lapped the corners and all intersecting joints using a router and put them together with a generous amount of glue. Note that the edges of the glulams are mahogany. The circle in the upper right of the picture below is a 16-gauge nail which didn't go in straight.

The glulam's were assembled into a frame the shape of the major parts of the door. Note the glue bottle with a roller. It was handy in putting down a lot of glue quickly.

The curved boards were done similarly but plywood was not used. Thin, clear pieces of a two by four were cut, steamed, dried, then glued and bent into place using clamps and brad nails to hold them in place until the glue set. Thin pieces of mahogany were also placed on the edges of the boards. They were also steam bent.

Then, one-inch mahogany boards were cut into two three-eighths inch thick veneers, with routed edges. These were glued over top of the glulam boards on both sides of the doors. Note all the blue pieces of tape indicating what each piece was suppose to be used for. It is easy to get confused with so many pieces to deal with, especially with two opposite doors.

After the door was assembled, small quarter rounds were cut on the router table and placed into the door as stops to hold the glass and plywood. I used plywood for the lower sections because code would have required tempered glass. Curved tempered glass cost $75 for each unique piece plus the cost of the glass and tempering. I decided that was too much. Maybe one day.

The glass I used for the double sliding doors was double strength window glass from the local glass supplier. I gave him a template and he cut the pieces. Some were a little oversized and I cut them back with a belt sander -- very carefully.

*Finished Product*

It took weeks to build these sliding pocket doors. As they had no hinges to minimize warp, I figured they had to be flat and stay flat. If I could have talked my wife into commercial doors, I would have. But, I can't deny the doors look good.

*Wine Cellar Door*

For some other doors, including the wine cellar door, a different procedure was used. It started with a commercial hollow door and three-eighths thick mahogany pieces were applied to it to make a door, which looked like solid and thick mahogany. For the lower panels, one-quarter inch mahogany veneered plywood was used. This was much simpler and faster than making the entire door. The edges were covered with one-eighth inch thick mahogany strips and the door looks solid. The door to the wine room had the top panels removed and replaced by glass. The pattern of the glass is bamboo as grapes were not available. If the backside of the door will never be seen, it could be painted instead of covered with wood.

A final requirement regarding doors is security. Largely, this relates to whether or not you use a door handle with a lock or not. That decision can be put off until the end and it can later be changed. If you use the same kind of lock as your house, you could have the lock modified to fit your house key, although in some cases, that may not be desirable.

One could also argue that the decision to install a window in the door reduces security to some extent. However, I would guess that the main concern is whether members of your household or frequent visitors, especially people under the legal drinking age, should have easy access to your wine cellar. For most people, the obvious answer is to provide a locking door handle with a key different from the house key. In some cases, a separate key-operated bolt may be a good answer.

Most locksets sold will work for a variety of door thicknesses; so, if you make your own door that is not a big concern. Just make sure your custom door is over one and three-eighths inch thick and not more than one and three-quarters inch thick. If you have to drill your own holes for the lock, special jigs are available to make it easier.


## Building Racks

### Vertical Racks

The first step in making racks is to prepare the boards. If you purchased rough lumber from the lumberyard, this means planing the boards to three-quarters of an inch thickness. If the lumberyard planed them for you, then the first step is to cut one straight edge on the board and you can skip the planing. If you had the lumberyard edge the boards, then you can skip that step and go on to making one by one rails and one by two stiles.

*Edging Jig on Table Saw*

If the boards are to be edged using the table saw another jig is useful. This one was made from clamps which are screwed to a piece of plywood, in this case I had a piece of MDO plywood left over from another project. Three clamps are provided to handle a variety of board lengths up to eight feet long.

If you are lucky enough to obtain leftover pieces of boards from your local lumber mill, you need to cut these to one by one (actually, three-quarters by three-quarters) using the table saw.

For a one-thousand-bottle cellar, the two thousand rails one foot long translate to two hundred fifty eight-foot long one by ones, eight feet long. For eight-inch boards, that means thirty, eight-foot-long boards. It is no wonder that people use many box racks instead of all vertical racks. By using two-thirds box racks, the number of vertical racks is reduced to a reasonable number of only ten eight-inch boards.

*Chop Saw with Stop*

Once the boards are edged and one by ones are cut to width, rails for the racks are most easily cut using a chop saw. In this case, a small piece of plywood is added for a stop to allow cutting five pieces at one time. Cutting more than five at one time from eight-foot long pieces is difficult.

*Board Sorting*

To simplify matters, the pieces should be put into boxes in an orderly manner so they can be retrieved easily later. Several boxes will be better to reduce the weight of each.

Assembling vertical racks is tedious, but simple. Any possible way to reduce the amount of labor or the amount of measuring required should be considered. The best of these is the use of a jig. In the pictures below can be seen a jig and a rack in various orientations.

## SIDE VIEW OF JIG

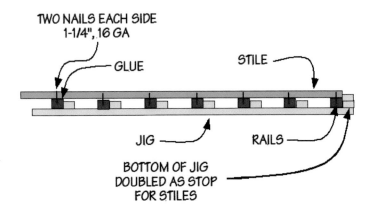

The steps are as follows:

1. Place the jig on a flat surface that will support its entire length. You don't want the jig to flex and produce a wine rack that is bent.

2. A full set of rails is placed on the steps of the jig.

3. Glue is applied along the front one and a half inches of each rail where the front stile will lie.

4. The stile is added and clamped in place.

5. Each rail is rechecked to make sure it is properly positioned.

6. Two finishing nails are nailed through the stile and into the rails. This would take a long time without a nail gun.

7. Excess glue is wiped off using a wet paper towel.

8. Glue is placed on each rail where the back stile will placed.

9. The back stile is set in place and nailed with two finishing nails.

# TOP VIEW OF JIG

TWO BY LUMBER
BLOCK FOR JIG
TO ALIGN TOP SIDE RAILS

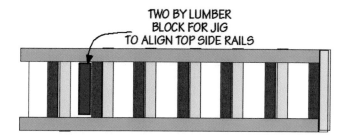

10. A two-by-four piece of lumber is cut and placed between the stiles as an alignment guide to set the top-side rails.

11. Glue is added to the each stile where the rails and stile overlap.

# SIDE VIEW OF JIG
### SHOWING ALL RAILS AND ALIGNMENT BLOCK

TWO BY LUMBER
BLOCK FOR JIG
TO ALIGN TOP SIDE RAILS

TWO NAILS EACH SIDE
1-1/4", 16 GA

GLUE

TOP RAILS

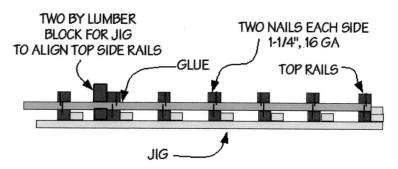

JIG

12. The rails on the top side should be added with glue and nails as on the bottom side. The blue jig was cut from a two by four to help in placement of the rails.

*Vertical Rack Jig in Use*

The rack below does not have a full set of rails on each side. This had to do with the layout of the room. Only putting rails on one side is required for a rack on the end of a set and the rails are omitted from the top of this rack to provide a place for the AC unit.

*Assembled Racks*

On each side, the cooling unit should be given three or four inches of free space to allow access for maintenance or replacement. Also, as the unit has a fan and maybe a compressor, there may be some vibration close to the unit. If a wood surround is placed around the cooler, it should not touch the cooler to avoid transmitting vibration to the racks.

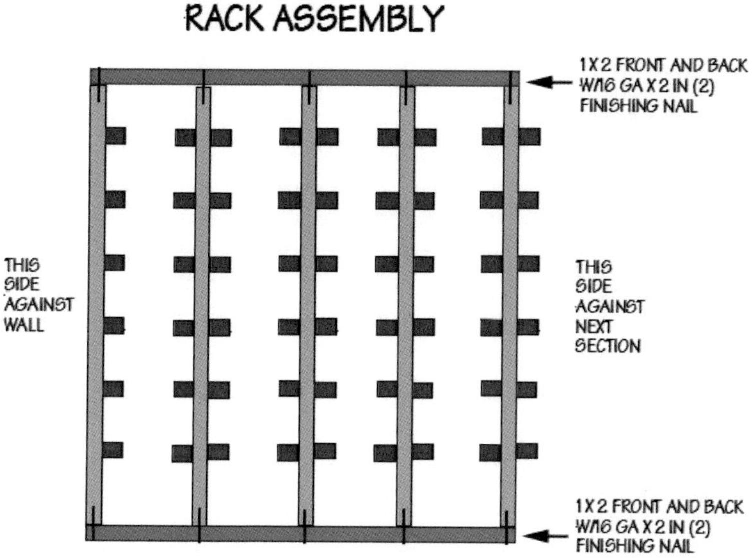

## RACK ASSEMBLY

1 X 2 FRONT AND BACK
W/16 GA X 2 IN (2)
FINISHING NAIL

THIS
SIDE
AGAINST
WALL

THIS
SIDE
AGAINST
NEXT
SECTION

1 X 2 FRONT AND BACK
W/16 GA X 2 IN (2)
FINISHING NAIL

*Vertical Racks Assembled with 1 x 2 Lumber*

Once the individual racks are assembled, they have to be connected into larger units as shown in the diagram above. This can be done several ways. The easiest way is to simply attach a one by two to the bottom and top of the racks in front and in back. A short piece of wood can be used as a spacer to get even spacing between all racks, top and bottom as they are being attached to the top and bottom pieces. The spacing I used was about three and seven sixteenths inches between risers.

A somewhat more sophisticated way to make the assembly boards would be to cut a dado (or groove) into the boards at the right spacing. This might most easily be done on the table saw with a panel cutting jig or using a router with a guide across a number of boards.

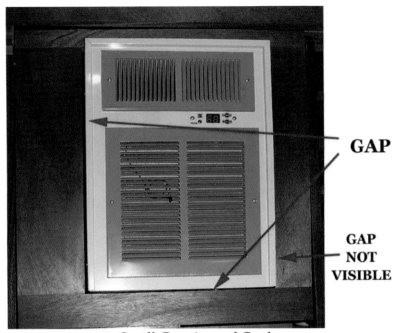

GAP

GAP
NOT
VISIBLE

*Small Gap Around Cooler*

Racks should be screwed to the walls with several screws that are long enough to penetrate into the studs at least an inch. Vertical racks can be grouped together with cross pieces that are screwed into the studs. The cross pieces should be firmly attached to each stud. An easy test is to grab onto each rack after it is installed and attempt to tear it out of the wall. If it comes out, it is not attached firmly enough.

## X Box Construction

The boxes are generally built with plywood, and plywood can be obtained in a variety of veneers to match whatever solid wood is chosen. Plywood is generally less expensive at around two to three dollars per square foot compared to five dollars or more for exotic hardwoods. Note that the edges of plywood will show in this arrangement. Several methods are available to cover the edges, including paint, commercial veneer, homemade veneer, and face frames, individually or in

114

combination. Boxes can be made individually or in vertical or horizontal groups. Plywood thickness of half an inch is adequate although if no face frames are being used, three-quarters may be more appealing.

# TRIPLE X BOX

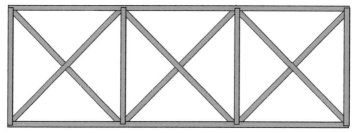

*Horizontal X Box*

In the example above, the horizontal pieces are cut to size and groves cut using a table saw, chop saw or router (or other hand tools) and the vertical pieces are inserted into the groves and glued and nailed or screwed. For places where the fastener will not show, flathead screws are preferred. They should be inserted into predrilled and countersunk holes to minimize the chance of splitting the thin plywood.

# BOTTOM PIECE DETAIL

The above detail shows slots (dadoes) cut in the horizontal pieces for the vertical piece to fit. Mine were done using a router bit and were cut three sixteenths of an inch deep. As half-inch plywood is not a half an inch thick, but only fifteen-thirty seconds thick, using a half-inch router bit will result in a loose slot. Router bits are sold especially for this situation by most companies online. In my case, some years ago, I bought a cheap router bit set which happened to have a fifteen-sixteenths bit. I don't know if it was done intentionally or if it was a metric, twelve millimeter bit, but it worked well.

The crossed pieces making up the X sections can be made from two pieces of plywood with a slot cut in each, similar to the way dividers are made in some wine boxes.

## CROSS PIECE DETAIL

To enable the cross pieces to fit neatly into the boxes, the ends should be cut at forty-five degrees from both sides resulting in a pointed end.

## CROSS PIECE END DETAIL

To get a beefier looking box, one can use a face frame. This is a frame made from one-by-two pieces and attached to the front of the box.

*Mahogany Edge Veneer on X pieces*

As this face frame has little mechanical strength requirement, it can simply be cut from pieces using square ends and attached to the plywood box with finishing nails. After finishing, wax sticks matching the wood color can be used to fill the nail holes.

In the previous picture, it can be seen that the front edges of the plywood X pieces have had narrow mahogany strips added to give the appearance of solid wood to the plywood and a face frame is attached to the top, bottom and edges of the X Box.

### Diamond Box Construction Detail

The diamond box is somewhat more complicated than the X box.

The best construction practice would have the angled internal pieces being placed into dadoes in the horizontal and vertical pieces and then nailed into place with nails angled into the internal pieces.

# TRIPLE DIAMOND BOX

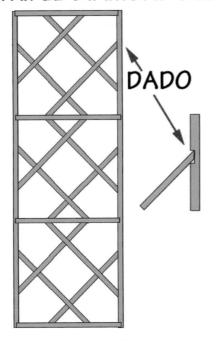

*Diamond Box Construction*

In this design, the four cross pieces in the boxes are cut as below and interlaced together to make the diamond box internal arrangement.

## CROSS PIECE DETAIL

Dadoes in horizontal and vertical pieces help hold the cross pieces in place as well as nails and glue. Veneer on the front of all pieces hides the dadoes.

118

## Finishing

Finishing has many implications. A nice finish makes the room look better and if a bottle were to leak or break, the wood would see less damage. Also, the act of dusting would be easier with a hard finish, although most of the wine cellars I have toured have never been dusted. Mine was dusted before the initial fill. The location where the finish is applied, as much as possible, should be somewhere else, outside or in a ventilated paint booth. Spraying the finish leads to a nicer finish, but a brush works well enough.

I've read opposing opinions on finishing wine racks. Some people think that the lingering odor will penetrate the bottles and ruin the wine. When I was taking a wine appreciation course at the local college several years ago, I asked the professor, a seventy-year-old gentleman with a PhD in biology, and a lifetime of making wine commercially, about finishing. He confirmed my opinion that whatever is in the cellar is not going to get through the capsule and the cork. Recently, I've seen several comments about tiny amounts of oxygen which diffuse through the cork and play a part in the aging process. As with most things about wine, there are differing opinions about this, also. The most authoritative opinion I've seen is that little or nothing gets past the cork. With that in mind, I recommend finishing the wine racks if for no other reason than if some wine leaks or is spilled, it will do little damage to the racks and cleanup will be much easier.

As a final point, my work is slow. From the time I finished the racks until the time the wine was added, weeks had passed, maybe a month in some cases. There was no trace of any odor remaining. Add to this the fact that the water-based poly had almost no odor to begin with and there is no reason not to finish your racks.

I have experimented with a number of finishes including shellac and varnish.

**Shellac** is easy to use and dries quickly as the solvent is ethanol. I have used a brush and foam brush and prefer a synthetic bristle brush. Each coat of shellac not only bonds to

119

earlier coats, but dissolves earlier coats to produce a single thick coat. Shellac comes in three colors, clear, yellow and amber. I thought the amber gave a nice yellow-brown tint to my mahogany entertainment center.

The problem with shellac is that it is not totally water resistant (although it resists short term water drops) and those white water-rings are common on some older furniture. Supposedly, coating the rings with alcohol will redissolve the shellac and remove the ring, but I have never tried it. Shellac is a good material to use to transition between finishes as it sticks to everything. It is also good as a sealer or a primer on wood. Some say that using shellac on pine will make stains less blotchy. I have tried that and it works, but not completely. The pine is still somewhat blotchy when stained.

**Varnish.** Among the varnishes, I have used three types: organic, polyurethane and water-based polyurethane. I used the organic varnish on most of my furniture projects and have had good experience with it. I have applied from three to nine coats of varnish with sanding between coats. For furniture grade finishes, after two coats, the varnish can be sanded with wet/dry sandpaper, preferably wet. On successive coats, grits from 320 to over 1000 produce a beautiful finish. For architectural items, I don't use that much care. With varnish on furniture, sanding is generally required between every coat to insure adherence. For wine racks, the pieces are not sanded unless they have planer or saw marks. Even then, sanding to 80 grit is enough, especially if you use a satin or flat finish. With gloss varnish, you may need more sanding.

I have limited experience with oil-based polyurethane. It is supposed to be the hardest finish commonly used and would be suitable for table tops and desks and any other surface expected to see lots of use or abuse. The sanding requirements are similar to organic varnish. Some woodworkers think that 'poly' is a new finish, made from chemicals and not as good as the organic original version. The truth is that 'poly' has been in use since the fifties and has been in use longer than most of the people who complain about it.

*Pre-cat Urethane, Sanding Sealer, Organic Varnish*

Recently, water-based polyurethane has become available. I resisted it at first, partly because I have little faith in water-based finishes, but finally gave in. (I use water-based paint for the house, largely because of the ease of cleanup.) Water-based poly has the counterintuitive advantage of drying to the touch quickly, in six minutes (less on a nice sunny day) and being ready to recoat in an hour. I have applied it with brush and spray and am happy with all the results. Painting the racks with a brush is tedious, but using a spray gun on vertical racks makes it an easy task. Using a High Volume Low Pressure sprayer from Rockler ($100 on sale), the varnish does not have to be thinned. For the boxes, the plywood was sprayed before the boxes were assembled and the boxes were touched up with a brush after construction was complete.

### Coloring

Regarding coloring the wood, the box racks are usually made from veneered plywood, although you can use solid wood and make panels. I used half-inch thick plywood and it appears to be adequately strong. If matching your solid wood is difficult or too expensive, veneered plywood can be used from other wood species and colored. I prefer dyes to stains as they don't accentuate the grain as much as stains. One of my first woodworking projects was an oak entertainment center and bookcases. I used a teak stain and the results were awful. The big pores in the oak absorb vast amounts of stain and can really stand out. It is anything but subtle.

*Teak Stained Oak Plywood*

By coloring the wood after the pieces are cut, many cutoffs are available for testing. I used a blend of a small amount of powdered red dye (the size of a BB), a similar amount of powdered orange dye and forty drops of liquid brown dye for eight ounces of water. To get to that point, I tested dozens of combinations. Note that you have to let the dye completely dry on the plywood cutoff, then apply a coat (or two) of varnish to really see what it will look like after it's finished. Also, whatever method you are going to use to apply the dye to the full size pieces should be used for the test pieces. You can't use a piece of paper towel to dye the test pieces and a brush on the full-size pieces and expect similar results.

Some people admire the ability to do it right the first time. I used to work for a company who rolled out a big campaign aimed at getting it right the first time. It was a disaster and was eventually dumped. Instead, I admire the ability to fix problems. I think that is better than being able to always do it right the first time, because that rarely happens. To that end, I have experimented with methods of recoloring wood to match other wood which wasn't colored right the first time. I first tried dying shellac. I put various dyes into shellac and then put those onto wood pieces which were too light in color. It worked fine the first time. But then, for the second coat, the new shellac dissolved the original layer and the first layer with color and it all blended together, ran and became a mess.

I gave up on coloring with shellac and moved on to coloring with the water-based polyurethane. This is much better because each layer does not dissolve the previous layer and just adds another layer of color to what is already there. Obviously, if you add too much color, you lose a lot of the wood look, but sometimes that is preferable to a piece of wood that is excessively light and stands out. Mahogany and others have a tremendous range of colors from almost white to as dark as walnut. I tend to keep the light colored boards aside and use them in places where they don't show or where dyed pieces won't be noticeable for their lack of grain.

The bottom line is that wine racks should be varnished and can be colored with stains or dyes if you don't use the wood species which has the color you want. I have read several books on staining and dying, and I believe that experimentation is the only answer. Likewise, if you find yourself in need of wood putty to fill a gap, try blending colors of putty and put those into boards on which you have made saw cuts. Let the putty dry and sand and varnish. Then decide which blend of putty was the best.

In all cases, experiment with cutoff pieces until you get what you want.


## Refrigeration

As previously mentioned, the obvious alternates for refrigeration are window/through-the-wall AC's, self-contained wine cooler units, split units and ducted units. Standard AC units and self-contained coolers mainly require a hole in the wall, access to electricity and possibly a drain line for condensate. I say possibly for the drain line because most standard AC units are made to entrain the condensate back into the hot air coming out the back, the condenser section. The window AC I used for eight years never had any noticeable condensate coming from it. It was designed to have the fan pickup water after it reached a certain height and throw it onto the coil where it evaporated. Also, the vapor line from the compressor ran through the pool of water and helped evaporate it. This, like everything else, has its good points and bad points. Putting the condensate into the air inside the house in winter might be good, but putting it into the air inside during summer would be bad, unless you live in a dry climate. In any event, you can always run a line from the AC to a floor drain or a large bucket.

*Split Unit AC Evaporator*

The instructions which came with my unit were quite clear. They said to get someone who knew what they were doing and pay them to do the work. But, as we all know, there is no 'expert' in DIY, but there is an I.

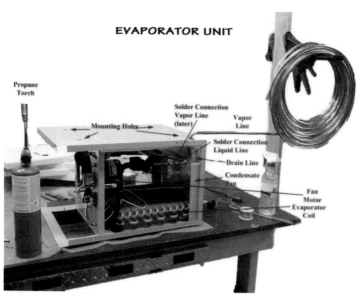

EVAPORATOR UNIT

Propane
Torch

Solder Connection
Vapor Line
(later)

Vapor
Line

Mounting Holes

Solder Connection
Liquid Line

Drain Line

Condensate
Pan

Fan
Motor
Evaporator
Coil

*Inside Unit, Evaporator Coil and Fan*

For installation of the outdoor unit, first it needs to sit on something. I used a twenty-four-inch square concrete paver obtained from the local building supply store. I first leveled the ground and then set the paver, making sure it was level and firmly set in both directions. Next, the inside unit was set and the refrigeration lines were run, making sure not to create any major low points or kinks in the lines. Oil will collect in low points and oil in the tubing is not as good as oil in the compressor. As shown in the picture, lines were attached while the inside unit was in the workshop. The lines were straightened and the unit brought into the house while the lines were fed through a hole in the floor, through the crawl space and through a hole in the rim joist to the outside, without creating any low points. Obviously a two-person job.

Insulation was added to the refrigeration return line before they were run. Also, it was cheaper to get copper refrigeration tubing as individual rolls rather than buy what they call a 'line set' which is a pre-insulated vapor line and smaller liquid line in a set. Six months after the unit was placed in service, we

125

where having a wet and humid summer. The vapor line began to sweat. I added water pipe insulation of the type with self adhesive joints. That worked and no more sweating.

Note that refrigeration tubing is slightly thinner than other copper tubing and the tubing size is the OD of the tubing. Another set of tubing sizes exists and does not match the refrigeration fittings. Make sure the tubing you get specifically says it is refrigeration tubing.

As refrigeration tubing is a slightly different size than other copper tubing, finding fittings was difficult. It turns out that five-sixteenths-inch tubing makes a perfect coupling for quarter inch tubing. Apparently, refrigeration technicians have a gadget which expands the tubing so that one piece of tubing can serve as its own coupling and the next can fit inside. It is probably called an expander, but I never ran across one and it would probably have cost more than I would like to have paid.

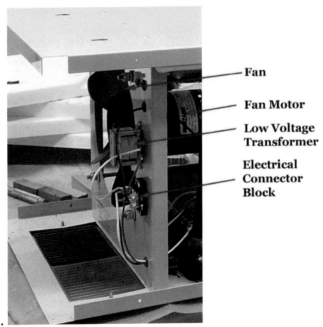

Fan

Fan Motor

Low Voltage
Transformer

Electrical
Connector
Block

*Inside AC Unit Components*

The picture above is a blowup of the inside unit showing the electrical parts. Note that the connector block where all connections are made. These include the 120 volt AC line to bring in power and the 24 volt AC line to the outdoor unit. The low voltage line is used to turn on a relay at the outdoor unit which turns on the compressor and fan in that unit.

The grill at the bottom of the picture is where the cold air exits the unit. The air outlet in this unit can be relocated to the top, should that be needed.

To solder tubing sections, a propane torch is adequate. If instead, you use a MAP gas torch, be careful not to overheat and dissolve away a piece of tubing. Many people on the internet recommend that acid free solder be used. The only such solder I know of is electrical solder. Avoid using the small diameter solder as it takes a mile of it to solder a joint. Some people claim that acid solder will corrode the tubing in the condenser or evaporator. On the other hand, some cans of refrigerant claim they contain additives to neutralize acids. Use acid flux solder at your own risk, but I doubt it's a problem.

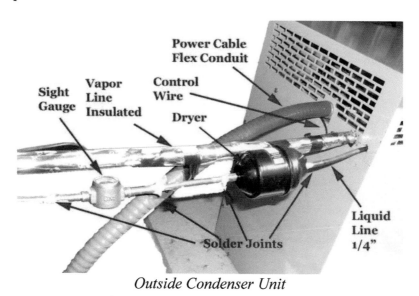

*Outside Condenser Unit*

My system came with a dryer and a sight gauge. Both had directional arrows printed on them and they are connected near the outdoor unit with short lengths of copper tubing.

An automotive gauge set was first tried to fill the system with refrigerant. Although the gauge set fit the refrigerant can (and would fit an automobile), it didn't fit the vacuum pump or the refrigerant connections on the outdoor unit. The connections on the outdoor unit, by the way, were Schrader connections with a built-in valve, like those on a bicycle tire. The connections on the vacuum pump had no Schrader valve but were otherwise like those on the outdoor unit. Then, a standard gauge set was obtained from a source on the internet. It was a first rate set with large easy-to-read gauges which also read vacuum and they cost the same as the cheap set I got at the local auto parts store. Live and learn.

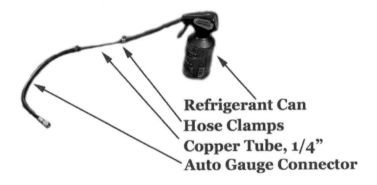

**Refrigerant Can**
**Hose Clamps**
**Copper Tube, 1/4"**
**Auto Gauge Connector**

The hose which came with a can of refrigerant was attached to one of the hoses which I got from the auto parts store using a piece of quarter-inch copper tubing with some hose clamps. The high-pressure hose from the good gauge set could have been used, but I didn't want to ruin it and the connectors on the bad gauge set were useless anyway.

*Refrigeration Gauges*

The good gauges were attached to the outdoor unit using the blue or low pressure hose. Then connect to the vacuum pump through the yellow hose. Both of the valves on the left and right of the gauge are closed. The vacuum pump had been purchased as a Christmas present the previous year from Harbor Freight. Refrigerant R-134a, as specified by the cooler manufacturer, is readily available at Wal-Mart and auto supply stores. Some varieties are even available with something called a leak sealer. That kind of leak sealer is aimed at softening rubber O-rings and has no value in a split unit. However, if you do end up with a leak, there is a leak stopper for sealing leaks in condensers and soldered joints.

The first step after soldering everything is to pull a vacuum to get rid of all the air and moisture in the system, although a major task of the vacuum is really to dry out the dryer. That takes time for the moisture to boil out of the desiccant inside the drier. One indication your new drier was wet is that it gets cooler during this process. Some say to hold the vacuum for thirty minutes, others say for two hours. So, open the left valve, turn on the vacuum pump to pull the vacuum, make sure the pressure is going down on the gauge and go have lunch. I left the vacuum pump on and it never got hot. My sight gauge had a moisture indicator which always looked green which meant the system was dry, but during the process, the color never changed. After pulling the vacuum, the valve on the gauge is closed and the vacuum pump is disconnected and the refrigerant can is connected to the yellow hose.

Make sure to blow out the air in the tubing before using it to add refrigerant to the outdoor unit. Start by loosening the connection from the refrigerant can at the gauge set. Turn on the refrigerant to blow all air and moisture out, then retighten the connection. Then the system is pressured to some low pressure, like fifteen pounds. Mix some liquid dish soap with some water in a plastic cup and brush it over all your soldered fittings to make sure you have no leaks. Watch the fitting for a few minutes to make sure there are no bubbles and that any bubble you made brushing on the soap doesn't get bigger. Then increase the pressure to forty pounds and check for leaks again. Let the whole system sit for an hour and check the pressure and leaks again. If you find a leak, blow down the whole system and resolder the connection that is leaking. Then, pull the vacuum again and pressurize the system again.

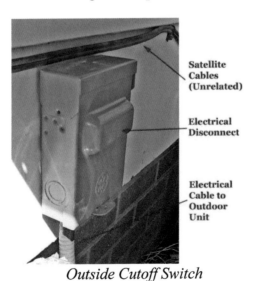

Satellite
Cables
(Unrelated)

Electrical
Disconnect

Electrical
Cable to
Outdoor
Unit

*Outside Cutoff Switch*

Once the system is tight, pressurize to forty pounds and turn on the electricity. The inside unit controls the outside unit so, it has to be plugged in first and then the outside unit turned on at the local switch you installed nearby. The code requires all AC units and similar devices to have a local cutoff switch. Generally speaking, I follow the codes not just because it is the law, but because it represents the accumulated experience of lots of people. (Using other people's experience is even better than using other people's tools.) On this switch, the electrical cable going to the unit comes through the wall through the rim joist and into the back of the switch. This avoids having to use another flex conduit.

*Sight Gauge*

My unit had a sight gauge, which I had to solder in place, downstream of the dryer. When the unit was filling, the sight gauge was clear and showed lots of bubbles, the gauge itself was only partly full of liquid and I could see the clear liquid moving through the gauge. Refrigerant addition was continued until the pressure was around forty-five psi. If the unit is installed in winter, it is wise to recheck pressures in the summer. Note that the lower the pressure, the higher the temperature difference in the inside unit and the higher its capacity to cool. On the other hand, if the temperature and pressure are too low (25 psi), the inside unit will frost over. Also, if the pressure is too low, the compressor capacity in terms of pounds of refrigerant compressed, will be lower. Less pounds of refrigerant moved through the system means less Btu's of heat are transferred. With part of the system working better at lower pressure and another working better at a higher

131

pressure, that means there is an optimum. That optimum is around thirty-five psi. At that pressure, the evaporator will not frost over and the compressor will pump a lot of pounds.

**Note:** During the installation process be careful when installing copper tubing as it easily bent into a pinch which could restrict the flow of refrigerant.

## Electrical

Before proceeding on this section, please note that electricity is dangerous even when you know what you are doing. I'd like to say I've been shocked more times than I remember, but that wouldn't be true. I remember them all and they were all bad experiences. If you only buy one other book before building your wine cellar, make it a book about electrical practice. If you are only going to buy one tool, make it an electrical tester, one with a meter or a light, preferably one with a meter. After reading the instruction manual on the meter, practice by plugging the probes into an electrical outlet. If you are not comfortable putting electrical probes into an outlet, you shouldn't be doing your own hookups. Also, check the codes in your area to make sure you are legal. If unsure, hire an electrician.

The electrical load of a room air conditioner compressor is not great for small units. These could be attached to an existing circuit if it is not heavily loaded. The load of the external unit of a split unit is also not great for small units, but can be considerable for larger units. A separate circuit is recommended for all but the smallest units. Note that many house circuits are rated for fifteen amps with newer circuits at twenty. Check the number on the breaker to be sure. If you use an existing circuit, your unit should pull no more than half of the allowable load of your circuit breaker and the amperage will be listed on a tag on the equipment.

For a split unit, the inside part only contains a fan and electronics and doesn't have a large electrical load. Mine runs at under two amps for the inside unit and eight for the outside unit, both at 120 volts. Check the manufacturer's data to be sure. In this case, the inside unit can easily use an existing circuit. If you live in an area with electrical storms, be sure to provide surge suppressors for the inside unit. Whole house surge suppressors can also be installed in the main electrical panel. Several manufacturers make a suppressor which looks like a 240 volt breaker and can be easily and safely installed by anyone knowledgeable in the workings of their main electrical panel.

The outside unit should be provided with a disconnect nearby for use during maintenance. The wire from the house to the box and from the box to the outside unit should be protected. A plastic flex cable covering is available to keep the wire out of the weather and away from animals. Provide a low point drip for any outside runs. Low temperature protection for the compressor may be needed in the form of a heating tape if the temperature falls below 20 degrees. Check with the manufacturer.

*Wires Sealed at a Top Plate*

Electrical cans in the wine cellar should be airtight to avoid losing cooling and should be rated for insulation contact to allow using maximum insulation. They should have the designation ICAT somewhere on the can or the box it comes in. When attaching a new fixture to an existing electrical box, watch out for air leaks. Most boxes are not caulked or foamed on the outside and hence leak air. It may be possible to put a small bead of clear caulk around the joint between the fixture and the ceiling or wall. For caulk, I generally avoid silicone as it does not seem to stick as well as acrylic. Some of the boards on my house, especially trim, were harder to remove because of caulk than because of nails I used to attach them.(In my latest six hundred square foot addition, I used four boxes, forty-eight tubes, of caulk before the rough-in inspections.)

*4 Inch Lighting Can*

The can in the picture is designed for new construction installation and has nails that are driven into the studs to attach it. Note that the ring around the outside of the bottom of the can is a gasket to reduce air infiltration. Even with this, I recommend caulking the joint where the can sticks through the drywall.

When working on existing wiring, always turn off power at the breaker as some electricians are highly innovative and find strange ways to wire a fixture or switch box to avoid using any more wire than necessary. Some of these methods have live power at the fixture even when the light switch is turned off. (I don't do that.) Be particularly concerned about three-way switches where the light can be turned on from two locations. There are many ways to wire these and most have live power at the fixture. Some people think that three way switches are misnamed because they turn on the fixture from two locations. But fixtures with one switch are called two-way switches because there are two ways for the switch to function, off and on. Three-way switches are off, on from here and on from over there.

Before turning off a breaker, turn the existing light switch on so that you can see the light come on and you have a solid indication that you have the right breaker. Then turn off the power at the breaker and go back and see that the light is turned off. Then turn the switch off. That way, if it is wired 'properly' you have two switches between you and the power. If not, then you still have the breaker between you and the power. If there is anyone in the house who might be 'helping,' put a piece of tape over the breaker, close the box and put a piece of tape there too, or even better, a lock and then put a piece of tape over the local switch after turning it off. I always follow this procedure and then carefully remove any wire nuts as if the power were still there. Then, I put a voltmeter on the bared leads without touching them to really make sure there is no voltage. Some pliers and screwdrivers have voltage sensing circuitry built in. Many of these are so sensitive, they will tell you there is power when there isn't. Use a voltmeter or a neon light instead. Working on a ladder is particularly dangerous because you might fall off the ladder because of even a small shock.

*Electrical Box*

Many kinds of electrical boxes are available. I recommend the deepest box you can get to make it easier to stuff all the wires and switches or outlets back into the box. Codes say that even for the deepest boxes, no more than three cables can be brought into the box. With that, it is still difficult to get all the wires back in without something coming loose or getting shorted. With three cables, it is usually necessary to use wire nuts to join all the wires together and a short jumper from the wire nut to the switch or outlet. Wire nuts make it even harder to get everything back into the box. Also, if your circuits are 20 amp circuits, all your wire has to be 12 gauge which is much harder to bend than 14 gauge used in 15 amp circuits.

In addition to the deepest boxes, I recommend the strongest boxes you can get to make sure the box doesn't get bent out of shape during installation. If the box is installed bent, making the switch plate look good will never happen. The boxes can be attached by several means. The most common is a nail at the top and one at the bottom. This is somewhat imprecise and pounding in the nails can distort the cheaper thin boxes. Also, several different variations of boxes with metal tabs are available. For existing walls, renovation or 'old work' boxes are available. These slip into a hole in the drywall and have screws that are tightened to secure the box to the drywall.

Another requirement of the code is to have a staple within eight inches of the box. This is to keep someone from pulling on the wire and putting tension on it at a point where it is bent. That could cause abrasion or an excessively tight bend of the wire and possible fires. The staples are also required every four feet in vertical runs and in horizontal runs where the wire is not running through a hole in the stud.

The picture also shows a hole in the stud, which was drilled before the wall was assembled. Holes were drilled in all the studs to make sure they were centered in the stud, which is required by code. I have seen many cases where electricians and plumbers have almost completely destroyed studs and floor joists to make room for their wires and pipes.

Another concern is that, usually, when you flip the breaker to disconnect a light fixture or switch, you are working in the dark. Working by flashlight can be done, but is not good. Two flashlights are better. I also have two lights which I can strap to my head (not at the same time, although maybe next time), but a better approach is to connect a extension cord to a working outlet and bring in a floor lamp of some wattage. I have an old torchiere lamp with a halogen 300 watt bulb which works well for ceiling work.


## Flooring

The installation of flooring can be simple or complicated, depending on the flooring chosen. A few of the many possible choices are listed.

### Vinyl

Vinyl sheet is simple and can often be found in home stores in precut pieces that can easily be transported in an SUV or pickup. Larger sheets are often cut to measure and may be rolled into a small enough roll to fit into a SUV or pickup. Vinyl sheets are often glued down, but it may be possible to simply glue or staple the edges and cover the staples with base moldings or shoe moldings. Vinyl tile is also available and relatively easy to install. Both should be installed according to the manufacturer's instructions, especially with respect to the type of adhesive and the type and notch size of the trowel used to apply the adhesive. Self adhesive tile with removable paper backing is available, but I have no knowledge of its long term viability.

The only vinyl I have used was in the garage as a moisture barrier for a number of cardboard boxes I was storing. It lasted the required five years and the only major damage was to the edges of the sheet, which were not secured. My parents installed vinyl tile many years ago and it lasted for the ten years we were in the house. It is necessary to make sure the underlayment beneath the vinyl has no bumps, as these will telegraph through the tile over time. Bumps in plywood underlayment occur at edges and edges can be tapered back with a belt sander or electric or hand plane. The taper should be long enough so that the change in elevation is not noticed, that could be a foot or more. An inch or two will probably not be enough unless the bump is less than one-sixteenth of an inch.

**Porcelain Tile**

Porcelain and ceramic tile are relatively easy for the amateur to install. Supposedly, an advantage of porcelain tile is that the color goes all the way through whereas on ceramic tile, the color is only on the surface. That distinction may no longer be true as the tile we installed had a varied color on the surface, but was a solid color all the way through. Small chips would not be noticed, but big chips probably would. Porcelain is supposedly made from better clay and is baked at a higher temperature to make it vitrify and have a solid, glassy and uniform consistency. In theory, it would not absorb wine through a crack. I cannot see that as a great advantage. A friend who worked at a construction site, years ago, recommended getting a car the same color as the dirt which would get on his car. He claimed that he never washed his because it was the same brownish color as the dirt. My car was

138

dark green and required weekly washing. The same advice probably applies to flooring. In addition, a varied color of tile of any color would show less dirt.

We installed tile in the office and in the entry and laundry room. Tile requires a stiff floor to avoid cracking. A single three-quarter-inch plywood subfloor is not likely to be adequate. I had a three-quarter-inch plywood subfloor and added a three-quarter-inch plywood underlayment with ten-pound roofing felt between the two. An auto-loading screw gun with three-inch-square drive screws was used to fasten down the underlayment. It was handy, but I wouldn't buy a special screw gun just for this project. A drill with a screw bit should be adequate for most wine cellars. The combination of the two layers of three-quarter-inch plywood made for a quite stiff floor. For what it's worth, stiffness is related to the cube of the thickness. A little thicker is a lot stiffer.

On top of that, I put down a layer of thin set cement (with flexibility additives) the size of the backer board and then the quarter-inch thick cement backer board. The backer board was screwed to the plywood with the screws recommended by the manufacturer. Backer board is cut similar to drywall by scoring and breaking and not by sawing. A special carbide hand tool is available for scoring. I got one many years ago and have used it for grout removal and other chores over the years. Also, some brands of cement backer board have a horrendous odor. A very chemical smelling odor and one I found almost sickening. For our floor tile, I used Hardiebacker board, which has no scent, but can only be used for horizontal surfaces. If you have to tile a wall surface, it isn't recommended.

Once the backer board is down, it is recommended to do a 'dry fit.' Place enough tile on the floor to make sure you understand your pattern. Also, consider the proper place to start the pattern. You want the maximum number of whole tiles to be noticeable and the minimum number of little cut pieces to be noticeable. Sometimes it is necessary to shift the whole pattern one-half tile over to avoid a little sliver along one side. It is preferable to have a piece larger than half on each side of a room rather than a sliver along one side, unless the sliver will be unnoticed. You have one chance to get the pattern right. This is it. Don't waste it. Do as much dry fit as necessary to make sure the pattern is what you want. Then, take a picture.

After the pattern is decided, use a chalk line to make lines all over the floor, every three feet or so. That way, you can make sure your pattern is maintained and many little adjustments can be made rather than one big adjustment that will look horrible.

*Dry Fit of Tile Arrangement*

Another layer of thin set was applied next. Only enough for four or five tiles at a time. If too much is put down at one time, it dries before the tiles are placed and the tile doesn't stick. Only enough thin set for about twenty minutes work should be made at one time. There is a special procedure for mixing the thin set and water is added to the bucket first. It includes initially mixing, then letting the cement sit (slaking) for ten minutes to cure and then mixing again.

I used a drill and a special mixing paddle to mix large quantities. I used a trowel in a one-quart yogurt container to mix small quantities. For larger quantities, a measured amount

140

of water goes first into a five-gallon bucket and then a measured amount of cement. I used an old bathroom scales to weigh the cement. (It got old as it was being used. Funny about that. Then it had to be replaced. I cleaned it up completely and it still works and looks good. Odd.)

The thin set was spread with a trowel with square notches. Trowels are available with different size notches on opposite sides. Read the directions on the thin set before buying the trowel. The thin set will provide directions on what size notches to use. In general, square toothed trowels are used for thin set with larger notches for larger tile. For hard to reach places, the thin set was applied to the back of the tile as well a thin layer on the floor. As each tile is set, it is checked for level against others around and for spacing from adjacent tiles. If a tile is not level, it must be removed, more thin set added and the space retroweled. By removing a tile, you can see if the cement is sticking and to what extent. For residential use, the cement should be in contact with around fifty percent of the back of the tile. For business use or high usage areas, eighty percent contact is recommended. The difference results from how hard the tile is pressed into the cement.

At first, we used plastic spacers between the tiles, but after a while, began to set them by eye. Drawing chalk lines on the cement board by snapping a chalked string is a good way to maintain the pattern over a long distance. Many different patterns can be used. If this is your first time in laying tile, I would suggest staying away from a pattern with lots of long, straight lines. Such patterns make small deviations easier to see.

As we tend to be perfectionists, we were concerned with the quality of the job we were doing. However, watching DIY shows on TV and looking at tile in commercial buildings, I think our efforts turned out well. It would probably be a good idea to have one person handling the thin set and the other setting the tile to gain the maximum benefit from the limited experience. In our case, my wife had no previous experience and set all the tile, doing a great job.

One of the criticisms I read of a previous book on building a wine cellar was that there was no discussion of how to level the floor in a basement. That seems a little far out, but I'll mention a few points, In one situation, we used an extra layer of concrete backer board under the backer board along with extra thin set under the backer board. However, in most situations, people use self-leveling compound, a cement-like product available at building supply stores. It is a very thin cement, almost like a thick tomato soup, and is poured out over the floor like water and allowed, like water, to find its own level with just enough spreading to get it where it needs to be. Heavy rubber boots and a hoe may be necessary.

I have seen numerous DIY shows where amateurs tried to apply self-leveling compound and did not read the directions. First, it has to be mixed precisely, according to directions, measuring everything, no guessing allowed. Second, when it says you have twenty minutes from when it is mixed until it is finished, it doesn't mean twenty-one minutes. And it means the whole floor, not just the first batch, has to be finished in twenty minutes. For a smaller wine cellar, this is feasible for the average DIY job. Mix as many five-gallon buckets of compound as you need and immediately pour them out. Two people may be able to do two buckets, but if you need more, then you'd better have help, all mixing at the same time and all pouring at the same time. Twenty minutes, that's all you get for the entire floor. Leveling a twenty-foot-square room this way would be a major effort requiring lots of people.

**Hardwood**
Floors of hardwood can be beautiful. Different styles from strip to laminated are available. Some types of floating floors come with an attached cushioning material on the back and can be clicked together quickly and easily without glue or fasteners.

142

GROOVE

BACKING

*Laminated Flooring*

We originally chose strip flooring for the living room as we liked its coloring and the ability to later sand it down, if necessary. Eight boxes were left over from the living room job and two were used for the wine room.

*Left-over Flooring*

Strip flooring is available as engineered or solid wood. The engineered wood is more stable and probably better milled, but the surface layer is thin and it can only be sanded once. Solid three-quarter- inch wood can be sanded several times which would be good for those who have slippery fingers and who do not like bottle dents on the floor.

Many different colors are available, but many are oak. Oak can have large unattractive patterns and if you stain it yourself, the pattern can get a lot worse. Some hardwood is made prefinished with a surface finish. This finish is extremely hard and usually results in a lighter color than would be had from applying varnish. That is good in that it is more difficult to scratch (but it is not as hard as you might think and it still scratches), but scratches and dings are virtually impossible to fix later without replacing an entire board. I have found no process for a decent touchup of a surface finish, in spite of much experimentation. Replacing a board in tongue and groove flooring is not easy.

Hardwood floors do not require the stiffness of the floor required by tile, but a three-quarter-inch plywood subfloor is recommended. Half-inch subfloors should have another half-inch layer of plywood added as underlayment. (Underlayment is just a fancy word for another layer of plywood.)

*3/4 Inch Strip Flooring*

Wood floors are available in many different styles, materials and thicknesses. Our local building code recommends that floors be at least one and an eight inches thick. (Keep to the code!) Using thin flooring over even a three-quarter-inch subfloor results in a thin and possibly bouncy floor and is not recommended.

Also, particleboard is not recommended under nailed-down hardwood, as it does not provide good purchase for staples or nails. It would probably be suitable under a floating floor. In my wine cellar, the previous floor was carpet, with five-eighths particleboard over half-inch plywood. The floor was twenty years old and the particle board had deteriorated and was crumbling apart. It had to be removed. It took two days and was tedious, but necessary.

There is some argument about whether cleats (nails) or staples are better. When I went looking for cleat flooring nailers, I had to go to the next town to get one. It seems that a majority of flooring installers use staples. One reason might be that, on a long floor where outside light goes across the floor at a shallow angle, small raised spots can be seen where the cleats go into the wood. For a wine cellar, this is not a problem. At the same time, buying a three-hundred-dollar flooring nailer is a large expense for such a small room. If I didn't already have the nailer and the flooring left over from my living room addition, I would probably have opted to use either a finish nailer or a floating floor in the wine cellar.

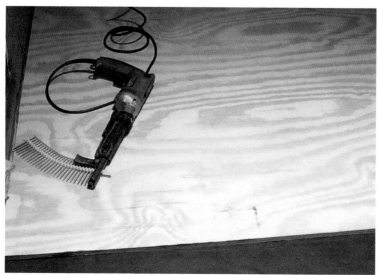

*Self-feeding Screw Gun*

The picture above shows a sheet of three-quarter-inch plywood in place over ten-pound building felt. The self-feeding screw gun was useful, but if it hadn't already been purchased for installing drywall and flooring, on another project, I would have just used a drill with a square drive bit for square drive screws. The phillips head screws normally available will not withstand torque as well as square drive screw heads. Three-inch screws were used to make sure the screw was long enough to go into the floor joists. The location of the floor joists was known from the nails visible in the subfloor and was marked on the walls before adding the building felt. The building felt was stapled down with a hammer stapler, but any kind of stapler or even tacks would work.

*Plywood Underlayment*

The picture above shows all the plywood pieces in place and screw heads can be seen. Note that the flooring will be installed left to right or along the long wall of the cellar. Therefore, the plywood was installed perpendicular to the flooring so that the flooring would be perpendicular to the seams in the plywood. Although the plywood was generally flat and elevation changes at the seams were minimal, a belt sander was used to minimize variations at the seams. Also, a one-eighth-inch gap was provided between plywood sheets to allow for expansion. A half-inch gap was allowed between the plywood and the walls or cabinets to allow for expansion.

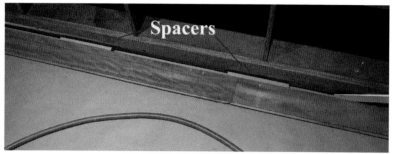

*First Row of Hardwood*

This picture shows the first row of prefinished hardwood strip flooring installed over rosin paper. Note that half-inch spacers (fancy name for pieces of wood) were inserted to provide space for expansion. (The spacers were later removed.) The cleat-type flooring nail gun was used to fasten the flooring down, but it is too big to be used on the first row. Nail heads can be seen near the edge of the first row. These are two-inch-long, 16-gauge finish nails installed with a nail gun. Similar size smooth finish nails can be purchased, but these have smooth shanks which provide little strength when in the subfloor. If the nails are to be done by hand, larger nails should be used, at least eight penny finishing nails. Also, the mahogany flooring would have to be predrilled to avoid splitting. As baseboards are to be installed, the nails will not be seen. A 16-gauge finish nailer is also used to nail through the tongue in places where the cleat nailer will not fit.

*Installed Hardwood Flooring*

In this picture, additional pieces of flooring have been added. Avoid having the ends of one row within six inches of the ends of an adjacent row. A bigger distance would be even better. Also, the rosin paper placed under the flooring to minimize squeaks and air leakage can be seen. Building felt can also be used. In my first experience with building felt, I overlapped rows of the felt. Later, I wasn't sure that was good as it varied the thickness of the floor because of the thickness of the felt. Rosin paper avoids the question altogether.

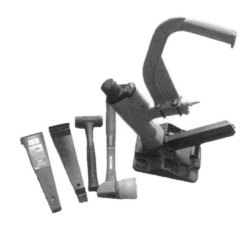

*Hardwood Flooring Tools*

The picture above shows some of the specialized tools needed to lay hardwood strip flooring. On the left are two pull bars, used along with the third item, a dead blow hammer to persuade the flooring to go where it's supposed to be. These are generally only needed near the walls where it would be impossible to use the next item. The big hammer with the plastic head is used to hit the flooring nailer causing it to push the flooring tight to the next row and then to inject a nail or a staple into the base of the tongue of the tongue and groove flooring.

If you've never done flooring before, it would be good to get some experience by nailing an off color or damaged strip into a thick piece of plywood. The plywood should be an inch or more thick, probably meaning that you need two thicknesses of three quarter inch plywood to keep the nails or staples from coming out the other side and damaging whatever floor you were practicing on.

*Final Floor*

This picture shows the finished floor with base molding attached. The base molding was custom made using a router table with mahogany wood.

## Tools

A number of tools are needed to make wine racks, depending on which type of racks are to be built. The basic materials of DIY racks are solid wood and plywood. The solid wood can be purchased at major building supply stores in dimensional sizes already planed and relatively straight and smooth. It is still wise to inspect each piece to make sure it is as straight as possible. Most sizes are three-quarters of an inch thick and are referred to as a one by lumber (one by two, one by three, etc.). The species of wood available at building supply stores are usually limited to pine, poplar, maple and oak. Pine and poplar are difficult to finish to a nice color, maple and oak are easier, although much of the oak has unpleasantly-strong grain patterns which get worse with staining. In this case, the sizes available are usually not the sizes wanted and tools are required to get everything to the shape, size and length desired.

For more attractive species of wood, one needs to find a good lumberyard. Most of my work is done in mahogany, as it is a hardwood with decent strength and is easy to work. I have done some work in teak which is oily and gluing can be difficult. It also quickly dulls saw blades due to contained silica. Oak, previously mentioned, is harder and more difficult to work for that reason. Wood at the lumberyard is generally delivered rough-cut. One can use a planer to plane off the fuzzy surfaces, but it only costs ten percent more to have the lumberyard plane it instead. They usually have higher grade planers which provide a smoother, more consistent finish, but it usually still needs to be sanded. Note that even if the lumberyard allows you to select individual boards (which is rare), the selection of unplaned wood is difficult. Even excessively light colors do not always show up.

The lumberyard I deal with also sells moldings in a variety of species. I generally make my own, but I will admit that even after hundreds of crown moldings, I still approach the process of making them with trepidation. It may also be possible, for a price, to get the lumberyard to cut your boards to the one by one or one by two sizes needed for vertical racks.

**Table Saw** - The vertical racks may be the most equipment intensive as it is difficult to make all the horizontal rails without a table saw. A table saw is usually used to make the rip cuts needed to convert wider boards into the one by one (actually, three quarters by three quarters) usually used for the rails. Stiles are typically one by two. Crosspieces used to tie the racks together can be one by one or one by two, depending on the style. Mine were one by two.

*Table Saw*

Considering that a 1000-bottle cellar using all vertical racks would require 2000 rails and around 100 stiles and dozens of connecting pieces, most of which are not available commercially, a table saw is a practical requirement. All of these pieces could be made with a handsaw, but the amount of work would be horrendous and the wine cellar would become a lifetime project. Most of us have better things to do, like drink wine (but never while using sharp tools). Also, instead of using one-by-one lumber for the rails, one-by-two pine or

151

poplar could be used with a doubling of the cost of the wood. Buying a low-cost portable table saw would probably be less expensive at around $200, than the additional wood. A better, contractor grade saw, at around $300, would be an improvement resulting in less sanding later. Upgrading to a cabinet saw would be hard to justify, but Sears sells a combination model at around $1000 which has a first rate fence. The fence is usually the downfall of cheap saws, but for several hundred dollars, it can be upgraded on most contractor saws.

For box racks, the table saw can be used to cut plywood into widths needed for the racks, although a circular saw in the hands of a good craftsman can produce a excellent cut. Cutting guides are available for use with circular saws that will help amateurs make better cuts in plywood. A saber saw (or jigsaw) can be used as well, but the cut edges will be rough and will require a great amount of sanding even when using a smooth blade. And of course, plywood can be cut with a hand saw, but will take much more time.

For those looking for the lowest cost vertical racks, one of the lowest cost forms of wood is the common two by four, preferably #2 grade instead of stud grade. A table saw could be used to cut these into rails and stiles. If a better appearance is desired, the pine can be dyed or stained (see finishing), but pine generally does not provide a good medium for coloring. The results, even when using a conditioner, are slightly blotchy. In this case, darker is better.

A final point regarding table saws is that a good blade is important. For furniture grade work, a 'cabinet grade' blade is useful and results in greatly reduced sanding. Such blades produce a far superior finish than the blade that usually comes with the saw. Generally, the more teeth the blade has, the better the finish, but at some point, arguably around fifty teeth, the finish is good enough and further teeth only slow down the cutting speed. Also, narrow kerf blades (narrow blades) require less power to cut the wood. This results in faster work, less burning of the wood and less wear and tear on the wood. (The only downside to thin blades that I have seen is that when using a table saw to make good edges on two pieces to be joined to make a panel, a thicker blade is stiffer and will make a straighter and tighter edge. For painted wood that isn't important and also, panels are not often needed in wine cellars.)

**Chop Saw** - A chop saw (sometimes called a miter saw) is used to cut rails and stiles to length and may also be used to cut sections of plywood to length. Its use for this purpose is relatively simple and the guide furnished with the saw generally provides sufficient instructions.

*Compound Miter Saw*

A sliding miter saw, which is slightly more expensive, will be necessary for wide widths of plywood. Chop saws all allow cutting angles, but angles are not required for racks unless you want a more finished end on the rails by mitering the ends. The chop saw can also be used to cut crown moldings and base moldings where angles are required. A more expensive version is the compound miter saw, which makes moldings simpler, but cutting crown moldings for odd angles can be mind bending. Charts are available on the web for the proper setting of a compound miter saw for various angles. Cutting crown moldings sometimes require an upside down and backwards approach, which is better described by a book on woodworking. I usually end up starting with some cutoff pieces until I get the procedure right.

A consideration with all saws is dust collection. Chop Saws are particularly difficult to make dust free. The picture shows a homemade arrangement for connecting a dust collector. It is under development and the next phase is under construction. When it's finished, it will show up on my blog.


**Router** - A router is basically a specially contoured bit attached to a high speed motor using a collet chuck. Routers are available from small units of around one horsepower to two-horsepower units which are the workhorse of hand-held units to three-horsepower units which are usually only used in a router table. Routers are probably safer than they appear, but a super sharp bit whirling around at twenty thousand rpm appears extremely dangerous. I've never been cut by a turning bit, but I am extremely weary where I point one. I have received cuts getting a bit out of a router. So, the router can be hazardous even when turned off.

A tremendous variety of bits is available for cutting various shapes into wood. The most common uses of the router is to make moldings such as crown molding, base molding and various edge moldings. In addition, the router can be used to make shallow grooves, or rabbits, in plywood to fit the various pieces together. Some woodworkers might also use a router to make groves in the stiles of vertical racks to fit in the rails for greater strength. Slots can also be cut in bottom and top rails to fix the spacing of racks.

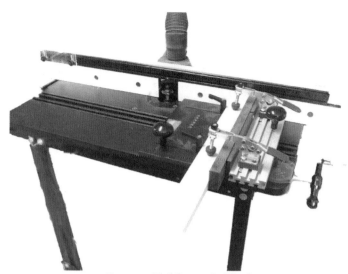

*Router Table with Sled*

The picture above shows a router table (router mounted under a table) set up to cut the end of a rail for a door or panel frame. A special sled is being used to hold the wood to insure a good square cut.

**Sanders** - The variety of sanders available is amazing, with most having specialized roles. I have four different belt sanders, two random orbital sanders (the family that sands together, stands together), a one-third page oscillating sander, a quarter-page oscillating sander, a pattern sander, four detail sanders, an oscillating drum sander, two disk sanders and I still haven't found one for every job I have and I still do far too much hand sanding. I always check the stores to see if there might be something better for those tedious hand-sanding jobs, like crown moldings.

The main unit I use for making racks is the random orbital sander. It is used to remove planer marks from the wood before cutting on the table saw and for removing saw marks on solid wood after it is cut. Plywood faces are generally not sanded as I usually use veneered plywood and the veneer is only a few hundredths of an inch thick. However, in the worst cases, one can use 220 grit paper with a light, practiced touch

155

on veneered plywood to remove shallow scratches. Plywood edges are usually sanded by hand using a sanding block (commercial or piece of scrap wood).

**Nail guns** - Most wood in racks is held together with nails. The glue I use, Tightbond III, is amazingly strong. Those parts I have glued with this material and which I have had to take back apart, invariably came apart by tearing apart wood fibers instead of breaking at the glue joint. It's great stuff, but I am a belt and suspenders kind of guy, especially when it comes to thousands of dollars of irreplaceable wine. So, the joints in my racks are all glued and nailed. In other words, each joint uses glue and at least two nails. Attaching two thousand rails to a hundred stiles with eight thousand nails can be done by hand. But it will take a long time. A sixteen or eighteen gauge nail gun with a small compressor can be had for $200 and makes the job much faster. The compressor can also be used for a framing nailer to make walls and a floor nailer or stapler for installing hardwood floors; so, It's a good investment.

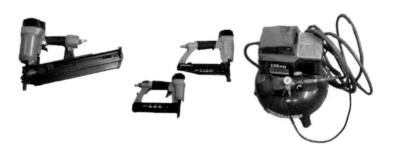

*Framing Nailer, Finish Nailers and Compressor*

The framing nailer shown above will handle sixteen penny, full head nails, the largest normally used in household framing, as well as smaller sizes. The nailer most used for the wine cellar was the 18 gauge finish nail gun. Nails come in a variety of lengths. This model will handle nails up to one and a quarter inches in length, which is fine for nailing two three-quarter inch pieces together.

The compressor is more than adequate for use with the nail guns. It is a little small if you intend to spray paint with a high pressure spray gun, but with patience can be used.

**Paint spray gun** - Finishing racks with a brush can be done and it is not terribly time consuming. Somewhat like painting a picket fence. Some people enjoy it, as it's a mindless task that allows the mind to wander to other more enjoyable pursuits, such as choosing, tasting and stocking a wine cellar. Some people hate it and would rather chew broken glass than paint a picket fence.

Using a paint spray gun to paint racks is easier and the finish is better than with a brush, at least in my experience. Also, painting the plywood is especially easier using a paint spray gun and you don't get any ugly brush marks. I purchased a high-volume, low-pressure gun from Rockler on sale for around $100. I think it was a good investment. It runs for hours without overheating and the finish is perfect. Before getting this spray gun, I didn't care for spray guns because cleanup is difficult and requires using a ton of paint thinner. If you don't immediately clean the spray gun, then goodbye spray gun. With a brush, it's goodbye brush, but brushes are far cheaper than spray guns. However, using water based finishes, including polyurethane varnish, makes cleanup much easier, doesn't require a trip to the store to buy paint thinner and doesn't smell bad. Also, the water-based poly dries to the touch in six minutes. So, on a cloudy day, spraying outside is not such a gamble.

**Vacuum Pump** - This is needed to evacuate the refrigeration system removing all the air and drying out the dryer before filling with refrigerant. I got mine at Harbor Freight. It is first necessary to fill the pump with oil, which is included in the box. The oil is poured into the compressor in the designated port before starting the unit. This unit ran for several hours altogether and never got hot. Also, it is quiet, making about as much noise as a fan.

I used a combination of pressure and purge to evacuate the system. I first pulled a vacuum and held it for thirty minutes, then pressured the system to fifteen pounds pressure, then released the pressure and pulled the vacuum again before finally pressuring to forty-five pounds.

*Vacuum Pump*

**Hand tools** - For the X box racks, I use a chisel and a Japanese saw to cut out the slots in the X pieces after they have been mostly cut using the chop saw. Any other saw would probably work, but the Japanese pull saw is easy to use and makes a thin kerf. Drills and screwdrivers are needed to attach angle and other braces to the racks to keep them in place in the event of an earthquake. We had one in most of the Eastern US a few years ago. I was in the worst possible place when it happened and I just had to 'sit' through it. Thankfully, there was no damage. Screws may also be used to attach rack sections to adjacent rack sections.

*Laser Tape Measure*

One of the more interesting and useful hand tools I have purchased lately is a laser tape measure. It works like the old sonic tape measures but is accurate to within one sixteenth of an inch. I have checked it up to around ten feet and it is accurate enough to use instead of a tape measure and is digital in case you have vision problems. The instruction manual claims it works to over one hundred feet, but I have not had need for such measurements.

While conventional tape measures are useful for outside measurements, they can be cumbersome for inside measurements, especially for those measurements greater than an arm span. This one has a variety of measurement modes. The one I use most of the time measures from the bottom of the device to wherever the laser spot hits. It also has modes to calculate area and volume, although I rarely use those. This is a great device to use for measuring studs that are to fit between top and bottom plates that are already installed, such as for a wine cellar in the basement or if you are adding a wall in an existing room.

159

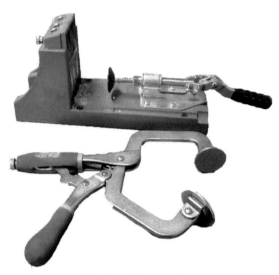

*Pocket Screw Jig*

An interesting tool for joining wood is a pocket screw jig, used with the clamp shown. Some years ago, items like the frame around the indoor unit of the AC would have been assembled using mortise and tennon construction. From there, the technology evolved to the use of wooden dowels and various doweling jigs appeared. I have a couple, but never liked them. Later, biscuits became common and I have three biscuit slot cutters now rusting away in my tool cabinet. I didn't like the idea of pocket screws even though a great many DIY shows thought they were great. Using pocket screws is unquestionably faster, but they just don't seem strong enough. But, finally, I gave in. I always use two screws or more for each end of a board and after a few dozen joints, they all appear to still be holding. For frames that have to be routed, I still use a panel cutting router bit set using the rail and stile bits. That system produces stub tennons which can be glued and which are quite strong.

# Chapter 6 - Operational Considerations

In general, a wine cellar requires little attention. Some exceptions are as follows:

## Temperature

Purchase a decent thermometer, independent of the cooling system and locate it where it is easily seen. Then, check it every time you enter the cellar and at least once every day you don't enter the cellar

The way to find an accurate thermometer is to look at all of them at the store and find several which read the same. Buy one of those. That works for mechanical thermometers, but not for digital as the batteries are not installed when they are sitting on the shelf. I have a glass laboratory thermometer I got many years ago and use it to check any thermometer I get. A high quality one can be purchased for less than twenty dollars from a laboratory supply store on the internet.

After I first wrote that paragraph, I broke my laboratory thermometer and started doing research on a replacement. As it turns out, many glass thermometers claim to have a low accuracy, plus or minus two percent of the reading, some say plus or minus two percent of the full-scale reading. Others say plus or minus two degrees. Some web sites say that digital thermometers are better with only a one-degree error. I checked five digital thermometers and they covered a range of five degrees F, no two having the same reading. So, how can we get excited about keeping the temperature in the cellar within a degree if we can't find out what temperature we have within two degrees? Recently, I have purchased a 'chocolate tempering' thermometer with a narrow range of forty to one hundred thirty degrees. It appears to be the most accurate thermometer I could get.

So, practicality says consistency is more important than the precise temperature as the precise temperature may never be known. The important point is that once you settle on a temperature, any deviation from that temperature signals a problem that should be checked.

## Refrigeration

Every time you enter the cellar, make sure the fan is running if that is the way you have configured your cooling system. Keeping the fan running will keep the temperature more consistent, especially in all those nooks and crannies. An indoor/outdoor thermometer placed outside the cellar, but with the bulb or remote unit placed through the wall inside the cellar would avoid opening the door unnecessarily, but then you wouldn't have an excuse to go into the wine cellar and admire your handiwork and your wine.

Recently, I have been experimenting with an Arduino, a single chip computer mounted on a printed circuit board the size of a credit card. I have been using it to monitor temperatures to find out what are the normal variations in my house and in the wine cellar. For those interested in programming and who are slightly knowledgeable of electronics, it is probably not difficult to construct a temperature controller for your wine cellar using an Arduino. The internet contains a vast array of instructional material and several books have been published about the Arduino. I mention this in case the electronic controller in your expensive cellar cooler goes bad. I suspect that a replacement system would be expensive, too.

In addition, I have reprogrammed the Arduino to keep track of the time the compressor is running. In April with outdoor temperatures in the high seventies, the compressor runs up to twenty five percent of the time. It did get up to sixty percent in the summer time and I added more refrigerant to the system. In a cold December day, it runs fifteen percent of the time. If you don't have an Arduino, then go to the condenser unit during the hottest time of the day and check how long the compressor runs and how long it doesn't. If your on time is more than seventy percent of your total cycle time (on plus off) then something is wrong or you need more insulation. By checking the sight glass you can tell if you need more refrigerant by looking for bubbles.

Once a month, check the surge suppressor you use to protect the unit. Most have some kind of pilot light to indicate it is still working. If the light goes out, replace the surge suppressor. Having said that, I have had over a dozen of these in my house for five or more years and the lights on all of them are still working.

## Numbering

Before construction is begun, have a simple and logical numbering system in mind. For example, if you only have the vertical rows, they could be marked with letters from A onward. The bottle position in the row, counting down from the top completes the location, such as RA7 for the bottle in Row A, the seventh down. X boxes can be designated with a B (or an X) with a number for the box and a letter for the location in the box. For example, B2T for the second box, and the top section in the box. Diamond boxes may a bit more complicated.

Then, in your cellar book or computer, you can put the location. If using a purchased computer program, check what format it would prefer for the numbers before making your final decisions on numbering.

*Stick-on Numbers*

At 'Michaels' hobby shop, we found an amazing diversity of letters, but few numbers. I complained to the cashier that this was the reason for children's poor showing in math, but received no sympathy. None the less, I found more styles and types of lettering there than in the same amount of time spent on the internet. I did find some gold colored plastic letters and numbers on the internet, which may have been a good choice. They were mounted on sprues like model car parts and were not expensive.

## Loading

When loading bottles into the boxes, make sure all bottles in each section are the same size and preferably the same shape . Otherwise, they may not be stable and may fall if jarred only slightly. Also, if you are transferring hundreds of bottles from previous storage, allow the room to get to the proper temperature first for a day or so and then load a half dozen cases a day, to minimize the opening of the door and excessive load on the AC compressor.

## Empty Spaces

In the sad event that you don't have enough wine to fill your cellar or in the happy event that you thought ahead and made the cellar bigger than your current inventory, some people recommend storing full bottles of water in empty slots to provide thermal momentum and make the temperature in the cellar more stable. It sounds like a good idea. In my case, I only had room left for a few more cases so I didn't bother with the extra water bottles.

# Chapter 7 -Compressor Replacement

Two years after the system was installed (and a year after this book was written), the author walked into the wine room and it was not cool. Panic. What to do? The fan inside was running and the temperature displayed on the evaporator (inside) unit was blinking, indicating an alarm condition. Outside, the fan on the condenser unit was not running. The breaker was checked and it was off. So, the breaker shut down the unit. No problem. Just flip the breaker.

After flipping the breaker back on and going outside, the unit appeared fine as the fan was running. However, the sight gauge showed nothing. The top was removed and a clamp-on ammeter was used to check operation. Either the clamp-on ammeter was badly wrong or the compressor was having problems. It showed forty-six amps for six seconds, then nothing. It appeared the ammeter was bad as the wire going to the compressor was tiny, maybe smaller than twenty gauge. It couldn't possibly handle forty-six amps.

As the compressor would run for six seconds and then shutdown and as the ammeter reading seemed beyond belief, the problem was thought to be the starter. A new starter was ordered for four dollars. The starter is a small relay which fastens to the side of the compressor and switches the motor windings from the starter winding to the running winding.

For the next three days, the house temperature was lowered to protect the wine. The new starter was installed as soon as it arrived, but the compressor still wouldn't run. The pressure gauges showed 75 psi with no change when the compressor came on.

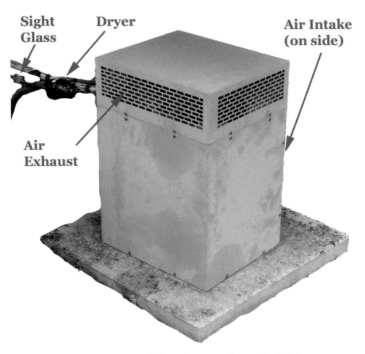

Sight Glass

Dryer

Air Intake (on side)

Air Exhaust

*Compressor/Condenser Outside Unit*

Part of the casing around the bottom of the unit was unscrewed and pulled back to obtain the compressor nameplate data. On the internet, dozens of places were found which sold that exact same compressor, (good news) but all were near Shanghai. (Bad news.) The compressor was made by SECOP, which is in China. Logical. Finally, the name Danfoss was noticed on the compressor. An internet search revealed two places which sold the compressor in the US. The first said 'delivery from the manufacturer in twenty days.' That one was skipped, knowing the manufacturer was half a world away. Five business days later, the compressor arrived along with a feeling of great relief. Unfortunately, four days of rain followed that, during which were many worries about seven hundred bottles of French wine.

## Preparation

The first step in doing anything is research. Everything which could be found on the web regarding replacing a

168

compressor was read. One video shows a guy with a torch, waving it all over the place and claiming it was easy to replace a compressor.

In fact, most of the installation of the compressor was simple, but it was constantly tedious and definitely unnerving. Too many possible mistakes. Too many admonitions that this or that had to be done precisely according to directions or hell would rise up and destroy the compressor and the wine.

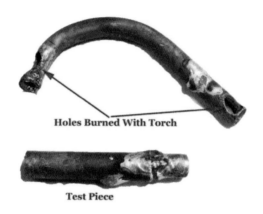

*Bad Brazing*

The only hard part appeared to be brazing, which was seriously unnerving, as holes kept appearing in the copper tubing. Don't forget that research not only includes reading, but also practice. A quick lesson on a leftover piece of copper tubing involved trying to melt braze metal on it, only after burning a hole in it. The best technique seemed to be to direct the flame onto the brazing rod and when it turned pasty, then concentrating the flame on the target. Soldering is generally done the other way around.

## Disassembly

After days and days of research, the sun came out and it was time to install the compressor. First, the top of the unit was removed, revealing the ports for adding and removing the refrigerant, R134a.

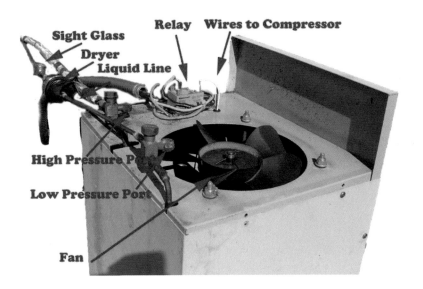

It is recommended (in various places on the internet) that refrigerant be removed before heating (soldering or brazing) the copper tubing as the temperatures involved could decompose the R-134a into acids. Some DIYers recycle the refrigerant into a used propane tank by putting the tank into a bucket of ice water. It would be necessary to pull a vacuum on the tank first, of course.

## Removing the compressor

After removing the refrigerant, a vacuum was pulled on the whole system and held for an hour. This was intended to, not only remove any refrigerant which could decompose into acids (they said), but mainly to dry out the dryer. It isn't known if the decomposition is reality or myth, but to avoid the possibility, a nitrogen tank was purchased from the local welding store. It cost $110 and was the second biggest cost, next to the $250 compressor.

After pulling the vacuum, the nitrogen was connected to the compressor gauges and the system pressured up. The salesman at the welding store said the regulator available was one made for regulating argon in wire feed welders (correct) and would probably only produce five pounds of pressure. He was reassured that would be enough. But, in actual practice, the regulator produced thirty-five pounds, close to the forty recommended for leak testing. It has a nut on the front, and perhaps it could be adjusted, should the pressure be as low as five pounds, but that wasn't needed.

After depressuring the system back to a few pounds, the valves on the top of the unit were closed. The valves are accessed by removing the cap (which looks like a hex nut) on top of the suction and discharge refrigeration connections.

The valves are then turned using an Allen wrench. Turning them clockwise closes the valve, isolating the compressor unit from the rest of the system. Turning them counter-clockwise opens the compressor unit to the rest of the system and is the normal situation. This was a way to avoid getting any oxygen or water into the dryer or tubing run or the inside unit when the compressor was removed, making it easier to evacuate in the future.

Next was removal of the middle section of the case to enable getting to the compressor. Otherwise, the compressor could not be removed because the fan motor was in the way.

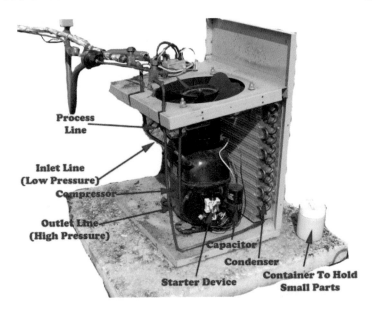

Interestingly, the middle section holding the fan was totally supported by the sides. It would seem that a few screws to the back would have been a good idea

Other than the compressor, fan and condenser, it can be seen that not much was inside the case. The compressor is the

172

big black tank with the white starting device and black capacitor stuck on its side. On the right side is the refrigerant condenser. Recently, when taking things apart, it has been useful to keep around a small container to hold small parts. It is wide mouthed for ease of access and white for ease of finding it.

Note that the compressor has a third connection, in addition to the quarter inch outlet and five-sixteenths inlet line. The third connection is a quarter inch fitting for a 'Process Line'. The Process Line is the connection through which the system is evacuated and filled when the compressor is used in a refrigerator. In this application, where separate high and low pressure connections are available, it is not needed and must be capped. In this case, the old tubing was unsoldered from the old compressor and used to cap the new process line on the new compressor.

The previous picture shows the nameplate of the compressor, containing the information necessary to purchase an identical replacement unit. Also, the process line is better shown.

After disconnecting the electrical wires and putting all electrical items well out of way of the torch heat, the first step in removing the compressor is to remove the tubing connections. I used an acetylene torch in reducing mode to heat the connections. They popped off easily, but with some solder attached. Instead of removing the solder, I used a tubing cutter and cut the ends of the tubing off. I tried removing the solder using the torch and a damp rag, but no luck. Cutting tubing with a hacksaw is not recommended as it produces small pieces of the tubing which could enter and damage the compressor.

This picture shows the wiring at the starting device and was taken, largely, to make sure how to reinstall the starting device. The coil for the relay can be seen on top of the starting device. A few years ago, the power company blipped the power and the kitchen refrigerator stopped working. It turned out to be the starting device. That one cost sixty dollars on the internet, but included half a dozen devices for various refrigerators. It was easy to install. At the same time, one of the wine refrigerators in the wine room also had a problem and luckily, one of the starting devices in the kit worked on that refrigerator.

Here can be seen the side of the compressor where the starting device attaches. It easily slips over the three pins. A black plastic safety cover snaps over the starting device prior to putting the unit back together.

The back side of the starting device has three holes where the three pins from the compressor connect. The starting device is pressed onto the pins and the wires are attached to the front. Removing it involves the reverse or simply pulling the device off the compressor.

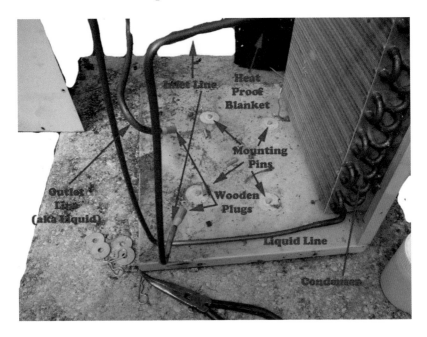

The old compressor sat on rubber feet secured with steel pins, steel sleeves, washers and cotter pins. Reusing the old pins was difficult; so, the quarter inch bolts provided with the new compressor were used. With the casing empty, it was easy to tilt it to the right and push the bolts in from the bottom.

Note in the picture, the heat proof blanket originally purchased for plumbing work. In this case, it was used to protect the top section of the unit from the heat of the torch while removing and replacing the tubing.

Also note the use of wooden plugs to keep air out of the tubing. These turned out to be useless as they kept falling out. Corks were considered, there was concern that little bits of cork would find their way into the compressor or into the capillary tube.

## Reinstalling the New Compressor

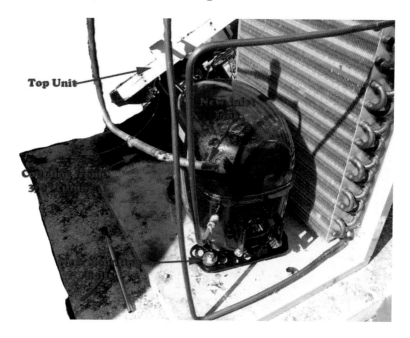

With the new compressor installed, a new inlet line was needed because of the hole burned in the copper tubing while trying to braze the old inlet line to the new compressor. The compressor has a steel connection which takes a lot of heat and the copper tube requires only a little. It's still not clear why conventional solder couldn't be used on these connections. It was assumed that greater strength was demanded by vibrating equipment. The coupling was soldered in with conventional solder after burning another hole with the acetylene torch. Such a procedure was actually recommended by several sources. The coupling was soldered with a MAP gas torch to avoid burning more holes.

## Startup

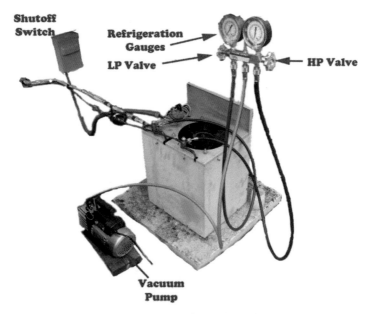

Shutoff Switch

Refrigeration Gauges

LP Valve

HP Valve

Vacuum Pump

Once the unit was reassembled, it was pressure tested with nitrogen and resoldered when leaks were found. Then, the vacuum pump (used for the original installation) was reattached and a vacuum pulled and held for an hour, after opening the valves at the refrigeration connections.

The unit was repressured with refrigerant 134a (Walmart) to twenty-five pounds and vacuum pulled once again. This extra step in the procedure was done to make sure all the nitrogen had been removed. Non-condensables are bad in a refrigeration system as they raise the condenser pressure and cost money in higher motor amperage and shorter motor life.

Finally, the unit was refilled to thirty-five pounds suction pressure. In this case, the stock of refrigerant ran out (two cans) at twenty-five pounds and it was necessary to buy more the next morning. Even at twenty-five pounds pressure, however, the evaporator was not frosting over and the system was cooling.

It took over a day to cool the wine room down seven degrees. The wine bottles required an extra day to cool the final degree. To measure the temperature in the bottles, an old port bottle was filled with water and a hole drilled in the cork. A digital thermometer was inserted through the cork and the bottle was set on its side at a place in the wine room where it was easy to see. The thermometer has an on/off switch and it is only turned on to check the temperature.

The new compressor performed as well as the old one, possibly better. One problem noticed before was that the unit was cycling often, every few minutes. The AC compressor for the house only cycled once every thirty minutes or so, at that time. It is possible this cycling caused the early death of the original compressor (one year warranty!). To lengthen the cycles, a one inch piece of copper tubing was taped to the temperature probe in the inside unit.

The company which makes the cooler sells a probe which fits into a bottle. This, no doubt lengthens the cycles and reduces starting and stopping. For that reason, it may be a good option. Previously, this option seemed wrong, because of concerns it would increase temperature variation in the wine room. Now, that variation seems minor and compressor life seems major.

## Conclusion

This whole episode has increased concern about the longevity and reliability of the cooling system. It was mentioned earlier that a backup unit might be a good idea. For split units, that cost would be a major consideration. Currently, a design is being developed which would use outdoor temperatures in the winter to cool the wine room and perhaps interface with a conventional air conditioner (cheap) for summer time use. Stay tuned.

In addition, this episode has increased the author's faith in DIY. It took about ten hours to do this work, divided into three days. Every hour which passed brought up a concern that this project would not turn out well. Possibly some tiny bit of dust or tubing or solder would enter the compressor and kill it. Perhaps the compressor didn't have enough oil. Or maybe the author's brazing skills were below par. They were. But in the end, it all works and has worked for two months -- and that's what counts. In fact, now the compressor cycles less often and it is hoped that the compressor life has been extended.

# Appendix

## Wine Myths

If you search the internet for wine myths, you will find some amusing stories, and it is recommended. You can quote these to your friends during dinner parties to get a laugh. Here, are mentioned only mention a few things the author learned over the years.

### Decanting

Some sommeliers in restaurants think that every red wine should be decanted. Some think that every red wine over ten years old should be decanted. Some think that decanting in front of a candle is a great show and they would decant bottled water if they could get away with it.

To make matters worse, some will walk up to the table holding the bottle like it was a pompom and they are head cheerleader at the Superbowl, waving it all around. If a wine needs decanting, it is because it has sediment. If it has sediment, then it shouldn't be waved around like a pompom. There is a certain amount of logic here that shouldn't be ignored. If one handles the bottles gently, then the sediment will stay where it was, even if it were on the side, which was the bottom while it was lying horizontally all those years. Also, once on the table, the sediment will tend to settle to the lowest point if allowed to.

My belief is to not decant anything, especially burgundies, as some flavor is lost in the process due to aeration. Instead, handle the bottle gently and watch for the time when you get to the bottom three inches of wine. Then, pour carefully and slowly.

## Different shaped glasses for different wine

A few years ago, it became common knowledge that experiments many years before showed that different parts of the tongue had taste buds for different tastes. As a result, wine glass makers began to make different glasses for different wines saying that each glass would make sure the assigned wine would reach the optimum point on the tongue. Many were quite expensive and most were quite attractive.

However, those many years ago, only one set of experiments was conducted by only one experimenter regarding this taste map and the results were held as true for decades. Later, when double-blind tests were done, it was found that all those glasses, while pretty and looking nice on the shelf, were not really useful. All regions of the tongue are able to sense all tastes. The best shape for wine is a snifter with a small opening. The small opening concentrates the aroma and that is the only effect which the shape of the glass has. So, get yourself a nice set of snifters to drink your wine and leave all those other pretty glasses on the shelf where your guests can admire them.

## Legs or Tears indicate wine quality

Some people believe that legs, or more recently tears, is a good index of wine quality. Long ago, I made a lot of wine and read that the legs were the result of glycerin in the wine. As a chemical engineer, the solution was obvious. So, I added some glycerin and my wine had great legs.

I even went to a noted French winery and sat as the owner, no doubt a double-digit millionaire, explained how the tears denoted greatness in her wine. But, alas, that has also been disproven. The tears look nice, especially after a glass or two, but have little value in indicating wine quality.

**Cheap wine causes headaches**

Some years ago, my wife noticed that if she had as many glasses of water as wine, then she never had a hangover. Some say that histamines in wine, predominately red wine, cause headaches in people who have a sensitivity to histamines. Other say, it is dehydration which causes headaches. That would be consistent with the idea of drinking a glass of water after each glass of wine. I could find no information which says cheap wine is any worse than more expensive wine, regarding headaches. If you have headaches, try drinking more water. At the very least, you will probably drink less wine and that will surely lessen the problem and cut costs. Some evidence also exists that taking an aspirin or ibuprofen an hour before drinking wine will reduce the headache.

As a final point, some people are allergic to components in wine and some people say that their migraines are precipitated by wine. Sadly, I doubt that water or anything else will help these poor souls.

# Reference Books

Listed in order of usefulness in my work

**General**
Housebuilding, A Do-It-Yourself Guide, R. J. Cristoforo

Do-It-Yourself Housebuilding, The Complete Handbook, George Nash

Working Alone, Tips & Techniques for Solo Building, John Carroll

Renovation, Michael W. Litchfield

Practical Housebuilding, for practically everyone, Frank Jackson

**Framing**

Graphic Guide to Frame Construction, Rob Thallon

Carpentry & Construction, Mark R. Miller, Rex Miller, Glenn E. Baker

Residential Framing, A Homebuilder's Construction Guide, William P. Spence

Structure, Roofing and the Exterior, Carson Dunlap & Associates

185

## Electrical

House Wiring with the National Electrical Code, Ray C. Mullin

Wiring a House, Rex Cauldwell

House Wiring Simplified, Floyd M. Mix

Wiring, Basic and Advanced Projects, Creative Homeowner

## Air Conditioning

HVAC, Residential Construction Academy, Eugene Silberstein

# Books by Taylor Michaels Publishing

~~~

## Non-fiction by Taylor Michaels
www.taylorjmichaels.blogspot.com

### Wine Cellar Construction:
### Tips and Techniques

### The World Traveler in Japan

### The World Traveler in France

### The World Traveler in Saudi Arabia, Bahrain, UAE and Egypt

~~~

## Novels by Taylor Michaels

### The American Wealth Wars

### The Sleeping Dragons of Texas
### or
### The Teardrop of Death

### An American Wizard

### The Cybot Wars
### Book 1
### The Alien Inside

### The Weak Shall Die: The Gathering
### The Weak Shall Die: Prepping
### The Weak Shall Die: Surviving
### The Weak Shall Die: A New World

**Mysteries by Sabena Stone**
www.sabenastone.blogspot.com

**Murder by the Clock**

**Murder in Emerald Hills**

**Murder by Lion**

**Murder of the Innocent**

**Murder One Too Many**

**Murder Along the Blue Ridge**

**Murder Among Friends**

**Murder Haunts Myrtle Beach**

19598702R00112

Printed in Great Britain
by Amazon